UNSHACKLING
DEMOCRACY

RealClear Publishing

www.realclearpublishing.com

Unshackling Democracy: Embracing Term Limits, Empowering Citizens

©2024 Gerrick Wilkins. All Rights Reserved. No part of this publication may be reproduced, stored in a retrieval system or transmitted in any form by any means electronic, mechanical, or photocopying, recording or otherwise without the permission of the author.

For more information, please contact:
RealClear Publishing, an imprint of Amplify Publishing Group
620 Herndon Parkway, Suite 220
Herndon, VA 20170
info@amplifypublishing.com

Library of Congress Control Number: 2023921957
CPSIA Code: PRV0124A
ISBN-13: 979-8-89138-087-5

Printed in the United States

This book is dedicated to the enduring spirit of our great democratic republic and to the citizens whose patriotism transcends the call of duty—those who advocate tirelessly for a government that represents the will of the people and not the tenure of career politicians. In the pursuit of a more perfect union, may this work inspire the reclaiming of our foundational principles through the adoption of term limits, invigorating the heartbeat of democracy and fortifying the promise of America for generations to come.

UNSHACKLING
DEMOCRACY

**EMBRACING TERM LIMITS,
EMPOWERING CITIZENS**

★ ★ ★

GERRICK D. WILKINS

FOREWORD BY RALPH NORMAN

CONTENTS

FOREWORD BY RALPH NORMAN 1
INTRODUCTION 5
CHAPTER 1 ACTON, ANGELS, AND ARCHITECTS 13
CHAPTER 2 A BATTLE OF PSEUDONYMS 33
CHAPTER 3 THE ROTATING PRESIDENCY 53
CHAPTER 4 THE CULT OF CAREERISM 73
CHAPTER 5 DOWN ON K STREET 93
CHAPTER 6 SENIORITY, INCUMBENCY, AND AMBITION 105
CHAPTER 7 PENDULUM POLITICS—WHAT CAN WE LEARN? 123
CHAPTER 8 LESSONS FROM MY WORLD 141
CHAPTER 9 ARTICLE V 157
CHAPTER 10 BUT WHAT ABOUT…? 171
CHAPTER 11 TERM LIMITS FOR THE SUPREME COURT? 179
CHAPTER 12 TOWARD A CONGRESS OF CITIZEN LEGISLATORS .. 189
NOTES 201
APPENDIX 207
ACKNOWLEDGMENTS 209
ABOUT THE AUTHOR 211

FOREWORD

BY RALPH NORMAN

WHEN I HEAR A MEMBER OF CONGRESS SPEAK AGAINST THE IDEA OF TERM LIMITS, I HEAR TWO THINGS. First, that person needs the job for whatever reason. And second, they want the job to be indefinite. No end in sight. But our republic wasn't built on that way of thinking, and it doesn't serve the rest of us very well. Government didn't build this country—people did. They still are, but not without more and more government getting in the way.

In the real world, away from my work as a congressman, I've worked as a real estate developer. Another successful man, Gerrick Wilkins, who is in the automotive business, has written the book you're reading. Both arenas are as tough and competitive as they come. I've made money, and I've lost it. Both are good things. You see, in the world outside the Beltway, you've got to be smart and learn from your mistakes. If you want perks, you must make them happen the old-fashioned way—hard work. But when you come to Capitol Hill as an elected member of Congress, you get treated like a king and can get pretty much anything you want.

But we're supposed to be working for the people and should be treating *them* like kings. After all, they put us here, and it's their money we're spending. Millions of Americans pay taxes just like Gerrick, and they want the government out of their lives, but instead, regulation and intrusion have been taken to a whole new level.

It's isolated and insulated here in Washington. And the longer someone's here, the more it becomes home. But it was never meant to be like that. That's why we need a book like this—to educate the public and remind us to return to fundamental values and practices.

And that's where term limits come in. We need them on Capitol Hill like we did 75 years ago in the White House. Because without them, Congress will never be fixed. And we know it will never fix itself. There are 535 people in the House and Senate, and we have the country's fate in our hands. But if the way things are done on Capitol Hill were transferred to the private sector—American businesses—those 535 workers wouldn't last long on the job.

So, Congress is not only isolated and insulated—it's immune.

If the men and women in the House and Senate had to rotate home after a few years, as opposed to staying here for eternity, and live under the laws and policies that come out of this place, things would undoubtedly improve. But that's not going to happen without term limits. Period. We need them to save our democracy. And we need them now. Careerism is killing the concept of representative democracy and our republic, and professional politicians are the ones with the weapon in their hands.

Commercial airline pilots are required to retire at age 65. That seems smart to me. I don't want someone in the cockpit whose reflexes have slowed with age. But we have members of Congress who are well into their 80s.

How does that make any sense?

Gerrick Wilkins's excellent book, *Unshackling Democracy: Embracing Term Limits, Empowering Citizens,* will be enlightening to some, validating to others, and encouraging to everyone. He makes the case for congressional term limits in a compelling and thorough way. I can't imagine anyone who reads these pages walking away anything but convinced that the time for serious term-limit reform is now. But I'm sure some will miss the point.

That group will be made up of members of Congress—and their staffs.

RALPH NORMAN (R-SC)
OCTOBER 2023

INTRODUCTION

I GREW UP IN FARMINGTON, NEW MEXICO, AND I'VE BEEN INTERESTED IN POLITICS FOR AS LONG AS I CAN REMEMBER. I enjoyed reading about great leaders even as a kid, books about men like Winston Churchill and Theodore Roosevelt. My favorites were those written about Abraham Lincoln. I remember being fascinated with how he stood against what was wrong in his day, even when his views and actions were contrary to popular opinion. I also greatly admired the greatest patriot of our day—Ronald Reagan—and his fight against the establishment.

One memory that stands out is from when I was in high school, and I heard Vice President Dan Quayle speak at our city's Civic Center. It was a major event for Farmington, complete with high school bands and drill teams. Because all 1,800 seats in the auditorium were filled, they had to broadcast his speech outside for the 2,000 and more who couldn't get inside.

Our U.S. Senator, Pete Dominici, was there, as were dozens of other officeholders and would-be politicos, including several

Navajos who supported the Republican ticket. The 1992 national election was just a few days away, and the Bush-Quayle ticket was in a tough fight for reelection against Democrats Bill Clinton and Al Gore, who were also in New Mexico, campaigning 400 miles away in Las Cruces.

I was too young to vote that year, but I remember watching the returns on television as the Republicans got what President Bush later called "the royal order of the boot." I liked that he used a Winston Churchill quote. During my high school years, I expanded my interest in politics and worked on a couple of local campaigns, one for a candidate for Sheriff and another for a candidate for District Attorney. During this time (1990s), discussion about term limits was gaining traction throughout the country, and this is when I first began to see the need for limiting congressional terms as a way to combat corruption.

My interest in politics ended up taking a back seat as I considered a career in Christian service. After graduating from high school, I headed to Pensacola Christian College in Florida. Faith is a vital part of my life. My wife, Carol, and I met at college in a political science class. I asked her out, but she turned me down. Then I asked her out again, with the same result. But I've always believed in the power of persistence, and I guess I made it my mission to get her to go out with me. The third time was the charm—she said *yes*. I later learned that her reluctance was because she thought my real interest was in a mutual friend who had introduced us in the first place.

Back then, my life plan was to get my degree and then go to law school, with an eye on a future career in politics, but as John Lennon said, "Life happens when you are making other plans." And the life that happened did not involve law or politics, at least not in a career sense.

Another Churchill quote I like is: *"My most brilliant achievement was my ability to persuade my wife to marry me."* We got married during my senior year in college. Carol was teaching in the speech department at our college as she finished her master's degree. I suspended my studies and took a job selling cars with a Honda dealership in town to pay the bills shortly after we got married. This was the beginning of an over 20-year career in automotive retail. Later on, I finished my undergraduate degree through Liberty University. After Carol earned her graduate degree, she went on to become an adjunct professor at Florida Gulf Coast University.

Not long after our wedding, we became active in the local Republican Party in Escambia County, serving on the executive committee. The first big political event Carol and I attended was Victory 2000 in Orlando, Florida—the state nominating convention. It was very exciting for us as newlyweds. Our governor, Jeb Bush, introduced his older brother, Texas governor, George W. Bush, who was running for the GOP nomination. It was quite a moment when "Dubya" told the crowd that the best thing he and Jeb did when they were growing up was to listen to their mother.

I was blessed to achieve success in the car business early in my career, and I rose through the ranks. My earlier ambitions regarding law and politics faded away as my passion for business grew. I was eventually transferred to Texas, and we moved to the Dallas area. During our time in Texas, I had the privilege of traveling to Washington, D.C., several times over the course of a year to attend the National Automobile Dealers Association Academy. My time there allowed me to become a more effective dealership manager, while also seeing firsthand the inner workings of our nation's capital.

Carol took a break from teaching when our daughter Hanna was born. She made the long-term commitment to use her teaching skills for the benefit of one student—Hanna. That homeschooling experience has informed our views on how parents should exercise their rights and choose the best educational path for their family. Throughout the homeschooling process, we discussed as a family the importance of limited government, individual freedom, and how our system of government works. My wife and daughter have both encouraged me to work on this book. I have no doubt we need more citizens to stand up for our country and provide necessary limits on government so our grandchildren and the generations to come can experience the unparalleled freedoms and opportunities our country has provided.

As my success in the business world continued, we made our way to Alabama. Though it was not somewhere we ever thought we would live, God had a better plan than anything we could anticipate. We've been in Alabama for more than 17 years, and we can't think of a better place to live. We love everything about it. Central Alabama is home.

During our years here, I earned my MBA from Samford University and now serve on one of its business school's advisory boards. I have also been a part of many ministries and church initiatives. I mention these because all of these experiences have informed my political philosophy and continue to convince me of the importance of term limits as something good for our country. I've been a conservative Republican from the start—embracing things like limited government and lower taxes. I'll share more about this in the pages to follow.

Though my career path put being a politician in my rearview mirror so many years ago, Carol and I have often talked about political issues, and she has consistently encouraged me to one day pursue my passion for the political arena. Hanna is now in college studying nursing at the University of Alabama in Huntsville, and Carol is working on her Ph.D. in adult education at Regent University.

During a recent missionary trip to Greece, working with E3 Medical Ministries and Crossroads Center, we both saw the plight of refugees. Carol has taken an active interest in helping people who've gone through trauma and is involved in assisting refugees to reengage in their education. She's got a big heart and has been my full partner in life and work. Every success in my business life has been possible, and any hope for success in any future endeavor *will be* possible, because of her.

One thing Carol and I keep coming back to in our conversations about the future—and this clearly springs from our experiences in business, education, and Christian work—is the idea that what Alabama needs, and the rest of the country for that matter, is more citizen legislators. By this, I mean people willing to answer the call of duty for a brief period of service for their fellow citizens. We see this as the best bulwark against entrenched and corrupt government—citizen lawmakers instead of career politicians.

It's an approach to public service for such a time as this.

I think most Americans want government to work, or at least to work better. But it's clear that we have major systemic problems and often find ourselves frustrated by how things get done (or don't get done) when it comes to the workings of various legislative bodies—from local town councils to state legislatures, and, yes, even to the U.S. Congress. One of the reasons for all the problems, particularly at the national level, is that people stay in power way too long. And the longer they're in office, the more entrenched our problems become.

But there's nothing new, as Solomon put it, under the sun. A famous quote from the nineteenth-century English historian Lord Acton will serve as a jumping-off point for what I'll have to say in the pages that follow. It's well-known, but I think too often ignored in the episodic debates about congressional term limits—*"power tends to corrupt and absolute power corrupts absolutely."*

It is clear to me that too much of today's political corruption is fueled by the simple fact that some hold on to power too long. In the coming chapters, I look forward to presenting a case for enacting congressional term limits. In my view, it is a critical step to reducing corruption, encouraging greater involvement in the political process, and restoring our republic to the greatness of the past.

Throughout this book, you'll find thoughts about my faith and how it impacts my political thinking. Let me be clear: I believe in the separation of church and state. But I also know that faith and politics don't always have to be in opposition; otherwise, the only people who could serve in political office would be those who have no faith at all. That's certainly not what the founders of our nation envisioned. They saw the value of religion as a force in society. John Adams put it this way: "We have no government armed with power capable of contending with human passions unbridled by morality and religion. Our Constitution was made only for moral and religious people.

It is wholly inadequate to the government of any other."[1] "And the man known as "The Father of the U.S. Constitution"—James Madison—was certain that "the belief in a God All Powerful, wise and good, is so essential to the moral order of the World and to the happiness of man."[2]

So, as a man of faith, I'm in pretty good company.

Separation of church and state has never been about the separation of faith from politics. Never. Back in 1960, when then-Senator John F. Kennedy ran for president, he did his best to neutralize the issue of his family's Catholicism. But in doing so, he made the mistake of suggesting his religion (which admittedly, was not a very big part of his life) would have no bearing on his politics. He was criticized by a Senate colleague named Eugene McCarthy—a man who would make his own mark on presidential politics eight years later.

Writing in a Catholic periodical, McCarthy said: "Although in a formal sense church and state can and should be kept separate, it is absurd to hold that religion and politics can be kept wholly apart when they meet in the consciousness of one man. *If a man is religious—and if he is in politics—one fact will relate to the other if he is indeed a whole man.*"[3] [Emphasis added]

One reason to factor in issues of faith when it comes to politics and policy has to do with fundamental human nature. The Bible teaches us that we are sinners and have a bias toward corruption. This is proven true every day—just read the newspapers or watch the news on television. If you start political equations with that as a bottom line (or common denominator), that will help you see the need for guidelines, even laws, to curb natural human passions and propensities. The Apostle Paul was thought to be one of the greatest spiritual leaders in history. He knew firsthand this struggle, as he indicates throughout his Epistles, especially in Romans 7:15, where he wrote, "For what I am doing, I do not understand. For what I will do, that I do not practice; but what I hate, that I do."

Without that realistic view of human nature—one revealed in Scripture and verified by empirical evidence every day—politics can tend toward the utopian. This tends to wind up becoming dystopian. Take socialism and communism, for example. They may sound good on paper, but they are inherently untenable. They have never worked and always wind up becoming tyrannical and totalitarian. Why? Because they don't factor in man's sinful nature—the reason power and corruption tend to live in the same neighborhood.

So, my faith will always inform my politics, not in the sense of trying to force my religion on anyone, but by giving me the kind of perspective that was dominant when men like Washington, Jefferson (yes, even him), Adams, Franklin, and Madison laid the groundwork for this great nation. As Benjamin Franklin, a man who was certainly not devout, put it during a heated debate at the 1787 Constitution Convention in Philadelphia: "I have lived, Sir, a long time, and the longer I live, the more convincing proofs I see of this truth—that God governs the affairs of men."

Indeed.

★ ★ ★

CHAPTER 1

ACTON, ANGELS, AND ARCHITECTS

"Power tends to corrupt, and absolute power corrupts absolutely."
—Lord Acton

THOUGH THE ONLY WORDS FROM LORD ACTON PEOPLE SEEM TO REMEMBER THESE DAYS RESEMBLE THE KIND OF SOUNDBITE COMMON TO X (FORMERLY TWITTER), there was much more to the man and what he said. John Emerich Edward Dalberg-Acton (1834-1902) was what we might call today a charismatic man. People were both attracted to and repelled by his magnetism, particularly his speaking voice. Listeners seemed to hang on to his every word. Because of his intense convictions, many saw him as a man on fire. He was a voice crying out in the wilderness of his times. His cry was about the dangers of political power. Acton correctly perceived that people in charge tend to operate out of self-interest and would always do what was necessary to hold on to power. He was wary of political power and saw it as more of an evil than anything good.

Deception, manipulation, and even the politics of personal destruction were the coin of every political realm. And political power was always the enemy of what he saw as the greatest good—freedom. To him, liberty was "the sign, the prize, and the motive in onward and upward advance." He didn't see it as a means to an end but "the highest political end" itself.

Though a devoted Catholic, he regularly faulted those who hid behind a curtain of religious authority. He saw no difference between religious or political despotism. He wrote his long since famous axiom about power and corruption in a letter to an Anglican priest in 1887, and I want you to see it in its larger context:

> *But if we might discuss this point until we found that we nearly agreed, and if we do agree thoroughly about the impropriety of Carlylese denunciations and Pharisaism in history, I cannot accept your canon that we are to judge Pope and King unlike other men, with a favourable presumption that they did no wrong. If there is any presumption it is the other way, against the holders of power, increasing as the power increases. Historic responsibility has to make up for the want of legal responsibility.* ***Power tends to corrupt, and absolute power corrupts absolutely. Great men are***

> *almost always bad men, even when they exercise influence and not authority, still more when you add the tendency or the certainty of corruption by authority.*[1]
> *[Emphasis added]*

Acton seemed to foresee the world as it would become not long after he left it, one where human government perpetually promotes itself as making the world a better place and its inhabitants happier souls. As a historian, he knew the past could inform the present and future. He died twelve years before the guns of August 1914 began to blaze. And when the smoke dissipated, the old world was gone, replaced by a brave new world marked by the evils of political power on steroids.

But exactly a century before Acton wrote the axiom that made him a philosophical immortal, a group of American thinkers and doers were getting ready to converge on the city of Philadelphia. Their task was formidable but clear—figure out how to create a republic that protects individuals from tyrannies to come and yet does so in a way that creates a government that cannot itself become tyrannical. They didn't have Acton's words to guide them, but they shared the same sentiments intuitively.

The Story of Us

From the start, our republic was about being free from tyranny. The brave souls who risked life and limb to proclaim liberty and then form "a more perfect union" were motivated by the idea that every person should be able to choose their own way free from government control. They foresaw the dark side of big government and left us a Bill of Rights as their legacy. They were suspicious of unchecked power and worked hard to create barriers to it. They were suspicious of concentrated power and tried to limit government wherever possible.

They knew something about human nature and political power's capacity to intoxicate. A sure way for someone to become power-drunk is to let him or her hold on to their bailiwick too long. Without a clear expiration date, an officeholder crossing the line between public service and personal fiefdom building is not noticed until it is too late.

Though he wrote it in Federalist No. 58 a year after their great collaborative conclave ended, I can imagine James Madison reminding those men tasked with creating a constitution for America, who gathered in Philadelphia's Independence Hall in the summer of 1787:

> *But what is government itself, but the greatest of all reflections on human nature? If men were angels, no government would be necessary. If angels were to govern men, neither external nor internal controls on government would be necessary. In framing a government which is to be administered by men over men, the great difficulty lies in this: you must first enable the government to control the governed; and in the next place oblige it to control itself.*

This is why, throughout our history as a nation, we have at times taken steps to mitigate the power of officeholders by limiting the number of times they can be elected and how long they can remain in positions of power. We've done it at the executive level for state governors and even the president of the United States, but there is a glaring outlier—Congress.

There are no limits on how many consecutive terms members of the House of Representatives or Senate can serve. Theirs is a system built around seniority and fiefdoms, one that has created powerful people who, for good or ill, have wielded national and even international influence.

This has been debated over and over, but this time, things may be different. Maybe term limits for members of Congress are an idea whose time has come.

Then—and Now

It's hard for us in this age of 24/7 news and hyperactive social media to envision what it was like more than two centuries ago, but "there were giants in the earth in those days." Great[2] men and great minds. They proclaimed independence and won a war. This might be enough for some, but more work was needed. Like the birth of a child, the story wasn't over. It had just begun. And like that vulnerable baby, our nation needed to be protected and preserved. It also needed to grow and build a life.

The child metaphor resonates with me, particularly when I reflect upon the miraculous birth of our daughter, Hanna. It was an extraordinary time in our lives. Carol and I had recently relocated to Texas after my recruitment by John Eagle Automotive, one of the nation's leading dealer groups. Our stay in Texas had spanned just a few months, and during this phase, my dedication to work consumed more than 70 hours a week at the dealership.

On July 26, 2004, Carol went for a routine follow-up exam to monitor her preeclampsia, a condition that required careful attention. Unfortunately, her blood pressure remained alarmingly high during the appointment, prompting the doctor to admit her to the hospital immediately. Even though her due date was still over eight weeks away, an emergency cesarean delivery became necessary. At that moment, I was at work, 45 minutes away, and focused on preparing my team for the high traffic that happens at dealerships at the end of each month. I received a phone call from the hospital and rushed to Carol's side.

As I navigated through the always congested Dallas traffic, my heart filled with prayers for Carol and our unborn child. A few intense hours after my arrival, our beautiful Hanna entered this world, weighing barely three pounds. That was the beginning of a challenging journey, as we spent extended periods in the NICU watching over Hanna with unwavering love and hope until the day arrived when we could finally bring her home.

Those initial days of parenthood strike me as strongly resembling the early days of our country. The mixture of joy, uncertainty, and exhausting responsibility of caring for a child mirrored the experiences of our nation's founders as they shaped this society for our parentage today.

Those great men put their minds together to try and figure out how to turn the child they had conceived into a republic unlike anything the world had seen. Turns out, the hard part was ahead of them. They were fighting against forces from history and the future, forces that seemed to mock their noble efforts.

As a case in point, less than two years after our Constitutional Convention in Philadelphia gave way to the venerable document that has undergirded our national way of life ever since, France—the nation that helped us cast off the chains of tyranny—found itself in a revolution of its own. But that story would play out in a very different way than did what Washington, Jefferson, Adams, Madison and company mapped out.

They gave us a republic with Benjamin Franklin's proviso, "if you can keep it." The French Revolution, however, though inspired by the hope of freedom, devolved into a vicious bloodbath that tormented citizens and created a pathway for Napoleonic despotism.

In fact, you'll be hard-pressed to find other revolutions, before or since ours, that worked out for those longing for better things. The very word revolution these days conjures up images of anything but people becoming free. From Russia to China to Cambodia to Cuba and so many other lands, revolution is a term of mockery and sarcasm.

Many things made our experience unique among nations, but significant among them was a collective determination to protect personal liberty and property by putting limits on government and public servants and, above all, to build political safeguards against anyone becoming a tyrant.

George Washington knew the importance of this as well as the temptations related to political power. Though he had been given the kind of unlimited power during the American Revolution that was akin to that of Roman dictators of old, he gave it back to Congress when the crisis passed. Then, after Yorktown and the American victory, his officers moved to establish a monarchy with Washington as king.

The great general quickly shot that down and ordered it never be brought up again.

A few years later, some military leaders sought Washington's support in a plan to use the army as a way to threaten the Continental Congress and strengthen the still-fledgling national government, but he condemned their efforts. Then there was that time at the end of his second term as our first president when he stepped down and initiated the first peaceful transfer of American presidential power to John Adams.

That so impressed a fellow across the pond that King George III, himself—the man who sent the "redcoats" to these shores—described his former foe as "the greatest character of the age." Washington was America's indispensable man and the catalyst for the beginning of the country we know and love. But not all would-be leaders wanted to be the same kind of noble and self-sacrificing man in charge. After his defeat and exile, Napoleon Bonaparte said, "They wanted me to be another Washington."[3]

Thomas Jefferson also got it. He understood "that even under the best forms of government, those entrusted with power have, in time, and by slow operations, perverted it into tyranny."[4] And a few months after he had added his signature to the Constitution that was now making its way to the states for ratification, he wrote a letter to James Madison citing some of his reservations about what they had recently created. Bear in mind that this was before Madison had begun to create his part of what came to be known as *The Federalist Papers*. Jefferson wrote about how he disliked "the abandonment in every instance of the necessity of rotation in office, most particularly in the case of the President." But it was not enough to keep him from supporting ratification. He told Madison that if the states approved it, he would "concur in it cheerfully."[5]

Of course, Madison, remembered as the Father of the U.S. Constitution, came out against the idea of "rotation in office" (how many referred to the idea of term limits back then), most notably in Federalist No. 53, where writing under the pseudonym Publius he argued against limiting terms for those in Congress because he thought there was a learning curve involved in developing enough knowledge to make good decisions. But it was an argument against annual as opposed to biennial elections—one-year versus two-year terms. He was worried that good men (read: those possessing character and knowledge) might not always be running things.

It is important to remember that these Founders and Framers were trying to think ahead, looking to an untested future, and trying to predict how things would play out. You have to wonder what the giants in the land back then would think about term limits (or rotation in office) now with the benefit of a couple of centuries of hindsight. These gifted yet flawed men were creating a new thing almost out of thin air. Thus, it's easy to find quotes from those who worked on the "Miracle at Philadelphia" that seem to put key figures all over the map.

Add to that how unlikely it was that the Founding Fathers would anticipate the extent to which lobbyists and special interests would influence the legislative process, a subject we'll examine in greater depth later in this book.

If It's Broke, Fix It

They had to go to Philadelphia for such a time because of the country's fragility due to a flawed, failed, and outdated document called The Articles of Confederation and Perpetual Union that had been crafted and approved by Congress in 1777. An effective wartime document, it fell glaringly short during the few years following the British surrender. The loosely confederated union it created was missing many of the elements we take for granted today. There was no provision for executive or judicial branches, and even Congress was unable to enforce laws or levy taxes. Everything was left up to the states—which might sound good to some these days—but the new nation was a breeding ground for disputation and rebellion back then. It was only a matter of time before something would set the political kindling aflame.

Then, in 1786, the fire was lit. Unable to provide for their families because of ineffectual and nonexistent financial structures, a band of former soldiers who had become farmers rose and began to protest, resulting in violence. It was called Shays' Rebellion, after Daniel Shays, a war hero who had fought at the Battle of Bunker Hill. The rebellion was soon put down, but it made one thing crystal clear to the men who converged on the City of Brotherly Love the next summer—we needed a stronger nation, a republic, with a clear set of operating instructions.

In other words—a *constitution*.

Though the old Articles of Confederation fell short on so many levels, there were a few things about it that continue to be relevant all these years later. First, that was what gave us our name, "The United States of America," right there in its preamble. The other thing about it is that it talked about something near and dear to my heart, which is the subject of this book—political term limits.

The idea of "rotation in office" was very popular at the beginning of "us." During the decades building toward Lexington and Concord, many Americans read something called *Cato's Letters*, a collection of articles and essays by a couple of British writers that, ironically, became an early influence on revolutionary thought in the colonies. These "letters" attacked political corruption and warned against the evils of tyrannical rule. The moniker, Cato, was a nod to the fierce enemy of Julius Caesar.

In Cato's Letter No. 61, we find these words that are directly on point with what this book is about:

> *But the possession of power soon alters and vitiates their hearts, which are at the same time sure to have leavened and puffed up to an unnatural size, by the deceitful incense of false friends and the prostrate submission of parasites. First they grow indifferent to all their good designs, then drop them. Next, they lose their moderation: Afterwards, they renounce all measures with their old acquaintances and old principles, and seeing themselves in magnifying glasses, grow in conceit, different species from their fellow subjects. And so, by sudden degrees become insolent, rapacious and tyrannical, ready to catch all means, often the vilest and most oppressive, to raise their fortunes as high as their imaginary greatness....* **A rotation, therefore, in power and magistracy, is essentially necessary to a free government.**[6] *[Emphasis added]*

It should come as no surprise that Article V of that constitutional forerunner had this wording: "no person shall be capable of being a delegate (Congress) for more than three years in any term of six years." It's obvious that the various elements of the old "articles" they sought to replace needed to be revisited in Philadelphia, and they were.

But what happened to the idea of term limits?

Back in the 1990s, though I was still in my teens, I followed the national debate on the subject of congressional term limits. And it made sense to me that the longer someone held on to power, the greater the tendency to become corrupt and complacent. Of course, that aligned with my views about human nature from my upbringing in church.

All these years later, I still feel the same way—but even stronger. Power is seductive and has a way of blinding someone's judgment. The district I live in has been represented by someone who has been in office for almost ten years. Before that, he was involved in other public policy endeavors. When he first ran for office, he told us he would commit to running for only five terms. But he has now changed his mind. His position is now that he can do so much for "us" by running again and staying in Congress. I guess he now regrets making that commitment. It shows me how the system can cause someone with good intentions to change their thinking. Politicians begin to think they are indispensable when in fact, they become consumed with their position and the power of that position.

It's a sadly familiar story; breaking such pledges seems more a rule than exception.

The Founders and Framers never envisioned people serving in elected office for *decades*. One reason is that the typical lifespan for Americans at the end of the eighteenth century was not even 40 years. It's twice that now. Good news for us. Bad news for Congress.

I believe fresh blood in Congress will bring fresh ideas. While working on my MBA, I did concentrations in *entrepreneurship* and *innovation*. These are very important concepts in the business world. Entrepreneurs fuel the American economy. Sure, big corporations seem to get all the attention, but small businesses create jobs and fuel economic growth in communities. Entrepreneurship is synonymous with the American dream. Car dealers are the epitome of entrepreneurship, and they constantly find new, innovative ways to make their businesses work better.

Entrepreneurship and innovation are flip sides of the same commercial coin. These fledgling businesses grow through innovation and invention. They are always looking for new ways to do things. I don't know about you, but that sounds like something Congress could use—innovation and the spirit of American entrepreneurship.

It might be helpful to think of Congress today as a large and archaic corporation. Out of touch. Isolated. Inbred. Like the Big Three automobile manufacturers back in the 1980s. General Motors, Ford, and Chrysler had been warned about the need to change their ways in 1973, even before an Arab oil embargo permanently changed the global economy. But they insisted on business as usual, that business being the building of large gas-guzzling cars long after the market for them had dramatically changed. It's a classic story of how entrepreneurship and innovation could have saved them from themselves, as documented in David Halberstam's classic book, *The Reckoning*—which should be required reading for every member of Congress.

Think about a company called Netflix. Started in 1997 as a service that shipped DVDs to customers, they delivered a billion DVDs ten years later. But things were changing, and they needed to innovate. Netflix started streaming videos in 2007 and eventually abandoned the DVD service completely. Now, they even create award-winning content. That's why you hear about them all the time.

It's also why you never hear much these days about Blockbuster, a now defunct video rental store chain.

Let's face it—most of the great things that happened in our country resulted from innovation in the *private* sector. Sure, there are reasons to be wary of technology companies getting too big and powerful. But when you think of things like the creation of the microchip, the smartphone, and other things we use every day, they've not come about because of government. We need government to referee things on occasion, but it can't create much on its own.

So why not make room in Congress for people who know how to get things done? The lack of turnover in Congress—something term limits would go a long way to change—means America is missing out on the benefits of having the kind of innovation we need for the challenges we face.

Back to Lord Acton

There is a clear connection between the tendency of power to corrupt and how long a person has had access to it. Let's be transparent—most of us have no problem with power in its proper place. Psychologists suggest we are wired for it. That aligns with something that dates back to our first ancestors, Adam and Eve. The instructions God gave them included having "dominion" over things. And though the first humans fell short when it came to so many divine instructions, the idea of subduing and control has stayed with us for good or ill. The original Hebrew word meant "to subdue." The context was for them to rule over fish, birds, and such.

But we moved on to other expressions of power.

People who aspire to lead others in the political sphere often have a higher need for power than many of their fellow citizens. Of course, all political leaders have a specific appetite for being in charge; otherwise, they'd stay home and skip the aggravation. But like a potentially addictive drug, having too much power for too long can change a person. It's been described as the "hubris syndrome." This, of course, is rooted in ideas from Greek tragedy and mythology and suggests that pride is inevitable and invariably invites destruction. Of course, the Bible reminds us that "Pride goes before destruction, and a haughty spirit before a fall."[7]

Have you ever noticed how often U.S. presidents behaved differently after reelection? Woodrow Wilson took us into a war he pledged to keep us out of. Franklin Roosevelt tried to pack the Supreme Court, and Lyndon Johnson got us mired deep in the muddy fields of Southeast Asia, even though he told the voters he wouldn't. Nixon had Watergate, Ronald Reagan had Iran-Contra, and Clinton, well, he had Monica. And you might remember what Clinton said about it candidly when asked why he did it. He said, "Because I could."

A compelling case can be made that even in a country driven by democratic principles, leaders can go off the rails. Thinking "out of the box" is good but doing so "out of bounds" is not.

The qualities most regarded as essential for effective leaders include the capacity to persuade, risk-taking, self-confidence, and vision. But too often, people who check all those boxes can be impetuous, reckless, and refuse to listen to the wisdom of others. Hubris rears its ugly head, and nemesis is somewhere down the road ahead. It tends to grow over time.

And the longer power is held, the greater the risk for power to corrupt. For politicians, it's actually an occupational hazard.

This is why most of the democracies in the world have limited terms for officeholders. Few leaders can survive more than a decade without the possibility of sliding toward the dark side and forgetting important values in favor of things that feather their nest. The goal becomes staying in power. Period. No matter what the rationale is, it has become all about them.

The bottom line is this: Power can be intoxicating. I don't think it's a stretch to suggest that some Washington politicos who have been inside the Beltway far too long are, in fact, drunk on the job, not with booze, but with the job itself and all its trappings. And like those addicted to alcohol or some other substance, they can't handle even the thought of living without their ongoing fix.

Before you dismiss this as just one more exercise in political reductionism, there is actual science that backs up what I'm saying. For example, Nayef Al-Rodhan, a neurosurgeon and neuroscientist affiliated with the University of Oxford, has written widely on the relationship between neuroscience and geopolitics. "Power, especially absolute and unchecked power, is intoxicating. Its effects occur at the cellular and neurochemical level," he says.[8] "The primary neurochemical involved in the reward of power that is known today is dopamine, the same chemical transmitter responsible for producing a sense of pleasure. Power activates the very same reward circuitry in the brain and creates an addictive 'high' in much the same way as drug addiction. Like addicts, most people in positions of power will seek to maintain the high they get from power, sometimes at all costs."

It is just another way to say that Lord Acton was right. So, in addition to the well-reported opioid crisis in America, something that rightly concerns all of us, there is another plague in the land—politicians addicted to being in office. And like other addicts, they will move heaven and earth to stay there and always resist attempts to limit their access to their drug of choice. They are hooked on the feeling of admiration, all those cool perks, and their overblown sense of importance and indispensability. And the longer they stay tethered to their drug of choice (political office), the more pronounced the addiction becomes, requiring more and more dopamine and more and more terms in office. Power eats away at their very souls.

How else can you adequately explain an 80-year-old man thinking he can serve another four years in the White House? Or how several politicians up the street on Capitol Hill who are even older than President Biden have the same mindset? They simply can't handle the thought of getting off their drug cold turkey. And because they are good at convincing people to continue giving them another chance—as are so many addicts—they seem to find a way to keep the dopamine flowing in increasing amounts through their brains.

I know that this analysis may sound harsh to some, but it's the truth.

There's another thing power can do. It can not only corrupt but is also reveals. Abraham Lincoln said: "Nearly all men can stand adversity, but if you want to test a man's character, give him power." And in a nod to bipartisanship, let me add something Michelle Obama said: "Being president doesn't change who you are. It reveals who you are."

Power has a way of exposing someone's true character,

and it also tends to fuel our flaws. And there is one thing for sure—how badly someone wants power or wants to hold on to it should be seen as a red flag. Power acts as a magnifying glass on the personality. So when people seek it or cling to it, we shouldn't expect them to behave differently than they did before. Jerks don't become servants when given power. They just become bigger jerks. Of course, not all politicians become corrupt over time, but they tend to compromise more. They have to in order to survive, so that in itself is revelatory.

Remember, the Founders and Framers had a different sense of human nature than we commonly find today. In *The Federalist* no. 6, Alexander Hamilton put it this way: "Men are ambitious, vindictive and rapacious." It's not a flattering description but one widely shared by his peers. But it's essential to understand human nature because it is the starting point of politics.

Human nature is the reason we need government.

And human nature is why we need to limit that government.

James Madison saw it in much the same way. He saw human nature as unreliable with a tendency toward hunger for power. He was determined to put checks and balances in place to ensure those running things didn't misuse their power. In *The Federalist* no. 51, he argued that "ambition must be made to counter ambition."

These men, and most of the others who got our republic off the ground, were students of political philosophy and the writings of the likes of Hobbes, Locke, and Hume. And they agreed with David Hume when he suggested that people in power tended to want more of it. Fifty years before our Constitution was drafted, Hume wrote: "It doesn't take as long for a ruler to become entitled to any additional power he may usurp as it does give him a right to a power that he gained all of by usurpation."

The Founders understood something too many Americans have forgotten, all the compelling evidence to the contrary. All human beings have a bent toward selfishness and pride, in other words, a sinful nature. I know that is not a pleasant thought, but it's reality.

Liberalism as we know it today is rooted in many ideas of the Progressive Movement from more than a century ago. In the late nineteenth century, there was much talk about how human beings were getting better and better. But then came The Great War, the Great Depression, and The Second World War, debunking the myth of human perfection. How often must the simple facts about human nature be dismissed?

Because we are all flawed, we need boundaries—like term limits.

CHAPTER TWO

A BATTLE OF PSEUDONYMS

"Those who hold office with a short tenure can hardly do as much harm as those who have a long tenure; and it is long possession of office which leads to the rise of tyrannies in oligarchies and democracies. Those who make a bid for tyranny are either the [demagogues] or else the holders of the main offices who have held them for a long period."
—Aristotle[1]

WHEN THE FRAMERS PUT THEIR SIGNATURES TO THE CONSTITUTION AND SENT IT TO CONGRESS, it was far from clear how the country would receive it. Part of this was due to the sheer surprise of it all. It was not widely known exactly what the convention had been working on for those summer months in Philadelphia. The official word was they had been tasked with making some revisions to the Articles of Confederation—which was widely seen as flawed. And their work was done far from the light of day.

Americans have always been suspicious of government-sponsored secrecy.

The proposed Constitution was published in its entirety in newspapers throughout the country within days of its release, and the initial public reaction was collective outrage. People saw it as something novel with elements like its description of a three-headed government. As the ratification process got under way, it was clear that whatever the tension and conflict had been like in that large room in Philadelphia, that was nothing compared to what was to come.

Early on in the process, citizens seized on some things that *weren't* there. One was a Bill of Rights to protect individual liberties. The other significant omission was language about the limits of personal power for those tasked with governing—in other words, rotation of office or term limits. With the memory of a fierce conflict still fresh in their minds, our early American ancestors were also concerned about anything that could lead them down a slippery slope toward *tyranny*.

The newness of our nation meant vulnerability. They knew the precedents in history and had real concerns that what they had fought for could collapse and that a single individual or group could accumulate power for corrupt purposes. Washington put it this way, "*The people must remain ever vigilant against tyrants masquerading as public servants.*"

More than two centuries later, it is easy to regard what we have as rendering us exempt from such a threat, but we're wrong. As Jefferson said, "*The natural progress of things is for liberty to yield and government to gain ground."* And it has been less than a hundred years since great democracies an ocean away gave way to tyranny so destructive that our Founding Fathers could have never imagined it as possible. We must never forget the words of one of our greatest presidents, Ronald Reagan: *"Freedom is never more than one generation away from extinction. We didn't pass it on to our children in the bloodstream. It must be fought for, protected, and handed on for them to do the same."*

The Great Debate

In order to help the young nation digest the proposed Constitution, a few of the men who had been present at its creation decided to argue its merits before the people at large in the most practical and public way possible. They would write serious articles for publication on the front pages of American newspapers. Those articles would come to be known as *The Federalist Papers*—a collection of essays supporting ratification, most of them written by Alexander Hamilton, John Madison, and John Jay, though under the pseudonym *Publius*.

So, what is today that old book relegated to civics classes and political science programs was front-page news and was not written for elites—but for everyone. My mind boggles when I think about how such brainy material would be received via today's media. Too big for Twitter. Too boring for prime-time television. And too complicated for TikTok attention spans.

Not to be outdone, a group of other men who had also been in the Philadelphia meetings created their own unique response to the work of Hamilton, Madison, and Jay. Writing under pseudonyms like Brutus, Cato, and Federal Farmer, their work was less organized and coordinated than their counterparts. They came to be known as the Anti-Federalists.

And remember, all of them—Federalists *and* Anti-Federalists—were Founding Fathers of our country.

Only ten days after the Framers finished their work in Philadelphia, a man using the pseudonym "Cato" told readers of the *New York Journal* that they should be wary of the new document, saying, "you ought to recollect, that the wisest and best of men may err, and their errors, if adopted, may be fatal to the community." Soon, a strong wave of opposition began to sweep the states. One man whose name is ever associated with liberty—none other than Patrick Henry—argued that the Constitution as written and proposed was "a revolution as radical as that which separated us from Great Britain."

The Anti-Federalists worked hard to create opposition in state legislatures. And sensing how effective their efforts were on the mood of the country, the Federalists realized concessions needed to be made in order for their brainchild to survive and be fully ratified. Madison went to the drawing board and, borrowing ideas from George Mason of Virginia, drafted a series of vital additions that would become the first amendments to what he had already fathered.

The Bill of Rights

It's hard these days to imagine the Constitution without it. It seems like nearly every great issue decided by the highest court in the land relates back, not to the Constitution as it was when it was signed in Philadelphia, but rather the first ten amendments to it. They have been a bulwark against tyranny throughout our history. And a strong case can be made that the attempt to ratify the Constitution would have failed but for the work of the Anti-Federalists.

How's that for forgotten irony?

We should therefore consider some other things the Anti-Federalists pushed for more seriously, particularly the idea of term limits. It was a familiar and popular criticism as our nation was being formed. A few years after his work on the Declaration of Independence, and as they were trying to figure out how to structure the fledgling nation, Thomas Jefferson strongly supported limitations on tenure. He said they were important "to prevent every danger which might arise to American freedom by continuing too long in office."

The Other George

Though remembrance of his name conjures up images of a university in Fairfax, Virginia, George Mason could be described as one of the forgotten founding fathers. But he should be remembered and revered. He and George Washington were friends, business associates, and Virginia neighbors.

As the colonies went to war with England, Mason helped craft the Virginia Constitution—particularly the Virginia Declaration of Rights, something near and dear to his heart. Jefferson drew from Mason's work when writing the Declaration of Independence.

Mason was a delegate from Virginia to what became the Constitutional Convention in Philadelphia in 1787, where he argued strongly for the inclusion of a bill of rights similar to those in the Virginia document. Because Madison and others overruled him on this, Mason was one of three delegates who refused to sign the final draft.

He also had reservations about how people would be represented in Congress. In his written objections to the final draft of the Constitution, he said, "In the House of Representatives there is not the substance but the shadow only of representation; which can never produce proper information in the legislature, or inspire confidence in the people; the laws will therefore be generally made by men little concerned in, and unacquainted with their effects and consequences." He wanted the kind of "rotation of office" the Articles of Confederation included as a way to ensure a close connection between constituents and legislators. He said, *"Nothing so strongly impels a man to regard the interest of his constituents, as the certainty of returning to the general mass of the people, from whence he was taken, where he must participate in their burdens."*[2] In other words, no permanent ruling class or political careerism.

Mason returned to Virginia and led the Anti-Federalist chorus of voices against ratification. Madison eventually agreed to support amendments making up a bill of rights because of Mason's pressure. Therefore, George Mason of Virginia should be honored and remembered as the Father of the Bill of Rights.

If only he could have gotten Madison and the rest of the gang to support term limits.

One thing that is often overlooked in any search for clues as to *why* the Framers of the Constitution seemed to lose interest in the original ideas of term limits could be the fact that most of those in Philadelphia were relatively young men with full careers ahead of them. The vast majority of the delegates were in their thirties, and we must wonder how many of them were thinking through issues with one eye on their own prospects regarding holding public office.

This may not seem fair, but it is certainly one central, unanswered question from those fascinating times. Could it be that some in that deliberative body didn't want to create strictures that might strangle their own hold on future power? We will never know.

But we do know human nature, a political factor as far back as Ancient Greece when Aristotle applied his massive intellect to political philosophy.

> *Such being our foundation and such the principle from which we start, the characteristics of democracy are as follows the election of officers by all out of all; and that all should rule over each, and each in his turn over all; that the appointment to all offices, or to all but those which require experience and skill should be made by lot; that no property qualification should be required for offices, or only a very low one; that a man should not hold the same office twice, or not often, or in the case of few except military offices: that the tenure of all offices, or of as many as possible, should be brief.*[3]

Conservative Principles

Conservatives have historically promoted and supported the idea of limited government, something directly related to term limits. They are the rightful heirs to our nation's founders when it comes to the concepts of concentrated power in the hands of flawed human beings.

After the end of World War II, the modern conservative movement became increasingly prominent. Historian Russell Kirk wrote a groundbreaking book in 1953—*The Conservative*

Mind: From Burke to Eliot. He went on to crystalize and popularize specific conservative principles.

> The conservative endeavors to so limit and balance political power that anarchy or tyranny may not arise. In every age, nevertheless, men and women are tempted to overthrow the limitations upon power, for the sake of some fancied temporary advantage. It is characteristic of the radical that he thinks of power as a force for good—so long as the power falls into his hands. Knowing human nature for a mixture of good and evil, the conservative does not put his trust in mere benevolence. Constitutional restrictions, political checks and balances, adequate enforcement of the laws, the old intricate web of restraints upon the human will and appetite—these the conservative approves as instruments of freedom and order.[4]

My thinking on these matters aligns with Kirk's thinking. And when you examine conservatism closely, you find clear clues that connect twenty-first-century American conservatism to a thread of history that dates back to the beginnings of Western Civilization—and even earlier. In fact, a case can be made that conservatism is the basis of Western Civilization. Maybe this is why the very idea of something called Western Civilization is under such attack during these revisionist days. Concepts such as the rule of law, tradition, faith in God, and passion for individual liberty are no longer popular among some Americans, even though they are, indeed, what have made America a great nation.

Those leaders who made things happen in 1776 and then again in 1787 were not only the founders of our nation.

They were the founders of the conservative cause. During the second half of the twentieth century, the heirs to those founders began to increasingly sound alarm bells about the drift of our country away from freedom and free enterprise and toward the kind of collective socialism dominating so much of the rest of the world.

By the 1960s, conservatives were a powerful cultural force, even able to nominate a man to run for president in 1964. Sure, Barry Goldwater lost to Lyndon Johnson in a landslide that was fueled, at least in part, by Americans mourning a fallen president, but from the ashes of that defeat rose the phoenix that would elect the great conservative Ronald Reagan just sixteen years later. Conservatism had grown from a movement of ideas to a movement of action, and ultimately to a movement of political leadership and governance.

Placing term limits on members of Congress is one way to bring the nation back to those heady days when conservatism was mainstream and sanity flowed through and from the streets of Washington, D.C.

The idea of limited government is closely related to the idea of innovation and how it has given us so many things to improve our lives. Why? Because the more government gets out of the way, the more creative Americans can be. Innovation involves the capacity to experiment and even make mistakes. Creativity works best in an atmosphere of freedom.

When people are free to experiment, and even free to fail, new things get done and broken things get fixed.

I am not anti-government. Not at all. In fact, my faith teaches me the need for human government to prevent cultural meltdown. We need a justice system because human conflict is natural. We need police because human nature can be greedy and vicious. We need national defense because the world is always a dangerous place.

But I agree with what Ronald Reagan said: "I hope we once again have reminded people that man is not free unless government is limited. There's a clear cause and effect here that is as neat and predictable as a law of physics: As government expands, liberty contracts."

Less government is better. We need to reduce it at the federal level to the lowest common denominator. If something can be done better by the states, then that's what should happen. Same with the county and city levels. Getting issues and problems closer to those they impact will breed more effective solutions. And the closer you bring issues to "home," the less chance there is for money to be a corrupting factor. You see, it seems that only the federal government and those who manage its purse strings (read: Congress) think they have infinite resources.

A Lesson from Forgotten History

What I'm about to say will outrage some, particularly those who prefer a revisionist view of American history. Here goes: the Founders and Framers had more in common with conservatives today than liberals. Now, even entertaining that idea can make someone from the left apoplectic. But, as I have already mentioned, they were students of political philosophy, especially those writers who wrote about liberty and rights. That thinking significantly informed both the Declaration of Independence and the U.S. Constitution.

They drew from two powerful movements that seem at first

glance to be at odds, but upon closer and more careful examination, form a potent hybrid that we can see in their thinking—the Enlightenment and the Great Awakening.

The Enlightenment was a European philosophical movement during the seventeenth and eighteenth centuries that impacted things like religion, art, and politics. Its primary focus was freedom. The movement significantly influenced the men who made America. They were immersed in its intellectual climate with ideas about natural law and rationalism. The latter is one of the reasons so many today assume they were anti-religious.

But, in fact, they were not.

Any careful reading of *The Federalist* reveals the influence of Enlightenment thinking. In Federalist No. 10, James Madison used Enlightenment ideas when he argued the merits of a constitutional republic versus pure democracy.

But as crucial as the Enlightenment was to our nation's founding, it's that other movement that contributed significantly to what was happening in the final decades of the eighteenth century. Historians remember that era as the Age of Revolution, as Enlightenment thinking fueled social and political movements to cast off the tyranny of monarchies and empower the people—citizens. All good, right? Well, it worked out great in North America.

But in Europe? Not so much.

Similar winds were blowing in France while revolution was in the air here in America. The American Revolution and the French Revolution are historically linked in our minds because they happened around the same time, give or take. But they were vastly different affairs. One led to a new birth of freedom, the other to terror and tyranny. That one also became the portal and model for horrors to come.

Both started with great words: America had "life, liberty, and the pursuit of happiness," and France had "liberty, equality, fraternity." Still, when we parse the words, we find some interesting clues about where we came from—and where we're going. You see, our deal here was about individual rights and dreams. Across the pond, it was about "the people" as a group.

And that is a significant distinction.

When Thomas Jefferson wrote about "life, liberty, and the pursuit of happiness" in the Declaration of Independence, he was borrowing, as I've already noted, from the seventeenth-century English philosopher, John Locke, whose triad was "life, liberty, and the pursuit of property." Jefferson's use of this language was clearly designed to describe the rights of individual people to live free, be free, and freely pursue their dreams in a free marketplace. Those thoughts were very much in presence in that Philadelphia birthing room.

In contrast, the French Revolution, though similar to what happened here in the sense of changing things and breaking free from an old order—had little to do with individual rights. It was all about collectivism—though that word was not yet in vogue. And in many ways, the French Revolution was the ancestor of all future totalitarian systems.

That's right, bad guys like Hitler, Mussolini, Pol Pot, and Lenin—and lesser political gangsters—were heirs of the revolution driven by Robespierre and company. We know this because the French Revolution, for all its ideological promise, eventually gave them Napoleon—who has been a common and inspiring hero to tyrants of all shapes and sizes ever since.

Rousseau had written about *volonté générale* or "general will," and the Jacobins, followed by others, ran with it, insisting that the voice of "the people" could best, actually only, be expressed by so-called enlightened leaders.

As I've noted, our revolution indeed drew a measure of strength from the Enlightenment. Still, the version of that movement here was influenced by something else—something that set the American Revolution apart from all the others ever since.

You see, the French not only declared war on the monarchy but also attacked Christianity, replacing it with a religion of the state, and introduced the worship of secularism. Sound familiar? Concepts like liberty, equality, and fraternity sound nice and make great propaganda. But in the end, without virtue born of something more profound and significant, it all looks the same. This is why totalitarian regimes call their realms the People's this or that—like the People's Republic of China or Democratic People's Republic of Korea. Vocabulary is important—but beware of those who use a different dictionary.

Words matter—but their meaning matters even more.

Why was it different here in America? The spiritual factor.

Now, I am not one of those who spends a lot of time trying to prove the Christian bona fides of our Founding Fathers, but I do believe that the influence of the Great Awakening, though it ended a couple of decades before Lexington and Concord, was still very much a part of our national fabric. Given this proximity in time and influence, it behooves us to pay more attention to its significance to our political emancipation. It has all worked and endured so well in this land because we are a nation "under God." There is no real liberty without that. Without a spiritual component, attempts at actual freedom move toward tyranny. I believe firmly in the separation of church and state. But absent a positive religious influence, a nation cannot long remain free.

Take the case of Thomas Paine—whose story is a cautionary tale. He wrote *Common Sense* in early 1776, which was vital to shaping public opinion in support of our patriotic ancestors. He was a revolutionary who helped us at a crucial moment. However, as he moved on and shared more of his thinking via his acerbic pen, he expressed ideas that, while probably resonating with some today, would not mesh with the spirit of 1776.

In *Common Sense*, Paine supported the ideas of freedom, small government, and even low taxes. But when the French got into the revolution game, his writings became increasingly radical. When parts one and two of his work, *The Rights of Man*, appeared in 1791 and 1792, he became a pariah in England and fled to France, where he was treated like a hero. They even made Paine an honorary citizen of their republic. But by this time, his writings advocated a progressive income tax, public works for the unemployed, and guaranteed minimum incomes. It's a lot like the standard Democrat platform.

Then there was his next bestseller—*The Age of Reason*. It was a rant against revealed religion. By his death in 1809, Thomas Paine was penniless and alone. Only six people attended the funeral of the man whose pen rallied America in the fight against tyranny.

I firmly believe that the concepts of life, liberty, and the pursuit of happiness, expressed individually (the intent of our founders), can only keep from drifting toward collectivism when there is a spiritual impulse—or at least a spiritual pulse.

A BATTLE OF PSEUDONYMS

I'm a big fan of C.S. Lewis and like how he put it in *The Screwtape Letters*:

> Hidden in the heart of this striving for Liberty, there was also a deep hatred of personal freedom. That invaluable man Rousseau first revealed it. In his perfect democracy, only the state religion is permitted, slavery is restored, and the individual is told that he has really willed (though he didn't know it) whatever the Government tells him to do. From that starting point, via Hegel (another indispensable propagandist on our side), we easily contrived both the Nazi and the Communist state. Even in England, we were pretty successful. I heard the other day that in that country a man could not, without a permit, cut down his own tree with his own axe, make it into planks with his own saw, and use the planks to build a tool shed in his own garden.

Five months after the battles of Lexington and Concord and the shot heard 'round the world later immortalized by Ralph Waldo Emerson, some Continental Army volunteers gathered at a church in the small coastal Massachusetts town of Newburyport—about 30 miles northeast of Boston. They were about to go to battle—an initiative led by, of all people, Benedict Arnold. The men decided that a little prayer accompanied by a sermon might be a good idea. Newburyport's Old South Church had recently received some notice as people proudly pointed out that the bell in its clock tower had been cast by a fellow named Paul Revere, who had a few months earlier taken his famous horseback ride, one that related to a certain Old North Church.

But a group of citizen-soldiers listening to Chaplain Samuel Spring that day knew they were also in the presence of another significant bit of history—something they saw as important to the emergent struggle for independence. As they listened to the sermon, many couldn't help but be preoccupied with the pulpit itself.

It had been the source of inspiration just after Lexington and Concord when the local minister spoke fervently about liberty. His passion prompted Ezra Hunt to step into the church's aisle and form a company of 60 fighting men on the spot—the first such group to attach itself to the fledgling Continental Army. But as if those two connections to the greater cause weren't enough, there was a third, even more compelling reason many men found the venue so fascinating.

It was what—or rather, who—was under the pulpit that really inspired them.

Five years earlier, a man who in 1740 had founded the Newburyport church came back to preach. He was, in fact, the most famous preacher in America—George Whitefield. By his 1770 return to the Old South Church, he had preached more than 18,000 sermons. But he died in his sleep in the church parsonage and was buried a few days later—right there in the basement of the Old South Church.

Because of the whitewash of history when it comes to the founding era, the story of Whitefield and the Great Awakening he helped spark has been sadly lost. Today's common revisionist narrative places faith and matters of religion on the periphery of history—an enduring lunatic fringe encompassing past and present. This better fits the secularist worldview espoused by those who want us to see government, statism, and struggles for social justice as not only the way to move boldly into the future but also as consistent with our past.

Sadly, such a future may, in fact, be ours if enough people don't wake up, but no amount of tinkering with textbooks can change what really happened way back when. The Enlightenment and passion that burned so bright during the epochal moments of our national gestation nearly two and a half centuries ago on these shores were fueled by something quite spiritual and profound. America may have been born in 1776, but it was conceived 35 years earlier when a handful of clergymen blazed like fiery meteors across the colonial sky.

And George Whitefield was the big kahuna.

A few years ago, a couple of Oxford-educated journalists wrote a book titled *God Is Back: How the Global Revival of Faith Will Change the World*. They made a strong case for the connection between the Great Awakening and the American Revolution. They saw it as "a unique event in modern history—a revolution against an earthly regime that was not also an exercise in anti-clericalism." They noted that the revolution in France "defined itself by its hostility to religion" but argued that "Americans saw no contradiction between embracing the values of the Enlightenment and republicanism while at the same time clinging to their religious principles."

Thank you, George Whitefield.

So, when the sermon was finally done at Old South Church that day in 1775, some of the citizen-soldiers sought out the church's sexton and asked to see where Whitefield was buried. The sexton opened the coffin, and a few officers obtained tiny bits of material from the dead preacher's collar and wristband.

Their simple excision of fabric was an exercise in

remembrance and connection. They knew that what they would soon do in battle was somehow linked to what Whitefield began years earlier. They were right.

Power un-tempered by spiritual values quickly gets out of control. Religion is, I think, like a control rod in a nuclear reactor—it protects from meltdown. Jesus talked about this when He called his followers the salt of the earth. Salt preserves against corruption. And I do not doubt that the Framers of our Constitution believed in the power of religious faith to curb human nature. They quickly added an amendment to it directly on point—the first one in the Bill of Rights.

The Founders and Framers greatly respected the idea of people living according to the dictates of their faith. But there is a tendency today by liberals to discount the importance of faith in our history and today. They prefer a more secular approach that not only abandons spiritual values but also dismisses them. But as Martin Luther King reminded us, "The Church is the conscience of the state."

And when government ignores religion, tyranny is never far behind.

Without the tempering impact of The Great Awakening, our revolution and subsequent development as a nation would have been the fruit of the Enlightenment run amok—as was the case in France. Secularism would have become America's religion, and the state would have become an object of worship. It would be like Supreme Court Justice Potter Stewart warned in his opinion about a ruling against prayer in the schools, seeing it "not as the realization of state neutrality, but rather as the establishment of a religion of secularism."

What does all this have to do with term limits? Quite a lot, actually. The very human tendency is toward control (power) and corruption. A view of government that does not take the proven-every-day reality of our common sinful nature will eventually find ways to rationalize totalitarian and tyrannical tendencies. In other words, without God—as Dostoevsky said—"everything is permissible."

The wise men who wrote our Constitution understood this. And if Madison and company could come back and see America now, they'd race back to 1787 Philadelphia and make sure term limits were the law of the land. Can you imagine how much better things would be?

By the way, there's an interesting footnote to that Newburyport-Whitefield story. In 1805, a fellow named William Lloyd Garrison was born there. You may remember him as a great liberator and abolitionist. You may not remember that the whole movement to abolish the scourge of slavery was set on fire by yet another great spiritual movement.

It was called the Second Great Awakening.

CHAPTER THREE

THE ROTATING PRESIDENCY

"Term limits would cure both senility and seniority, both terrible legislative diseases."
—Harry Truman

THOUGH HE HAD ONLY RECENTLY BEEN REELECTED IN A LANDSLIDE ON NOVEMBER 3, 1936, winning 46 of 48 states with a popular vote of more than 60%, 1937 was turning out to be a bad year for President Franklin D. Roosevelt. Thinking he had a mandate for pretty much whatever he wanted to do, his plan to "pack" the Supreme Court had hit a brick wall. A thinly veiled attempt to change the judicial dynamics of the court, the initiative quickly became a political bridge too far and tarnished the image of the man many saw as more of a savior than a politician.

And then there was the *economy*.

The nation that was just beginning to emerge from the depths of the Great Depression went into one of the worst recessions in a generation. Though not as severe as what started back in 1929, it was bad enough to cause confidence in the president's legendary political and policy prowess to wane. The downturn would soon come to be known as "the Roosevelt Recession." It should come as no surprise, therefore, that criticism of Roosevelt, once a risky proposition, became a national pastime for journalists and even entertainers.

These days, political satire and mockery of presidents is the norm. From the days of Chevy Chase as President Gerald Ford to these days of X (formerly Twitter) and TikTok, making fun of occupants of the Oval Office is always in fashion. We are accustomed to seeing our leaders portrayed as buffoons—or worse. However, such things did not happen in the days when the entertainment media was limited to radio and the theater.

That changed on November 2, 1937.

New York's *Music Box Theater* was packed to the rafters in anticipation of the opening curtain for a new musical, *I'd Rather Be Right*. It featured the legendary showman George M. Cohan as a singing and dancing President Franklin Delano Roosevelt. With lyrics like:

> *When I was courting Eleanor,*
> *I told her uncle Teddy,*
> *I wouldn't run for President,*
> *Unless the job was ready.*[1]

It was a cutting-edge (for the times) expression of political satire and featured FDR solving problems for everyday Americans. Though the audience received it well, one brief moment elicited loud boos from those in the expensive orchestra seats and cheers from the balcony. A tap-dancing Roosevelt sang, "Hang on to your hats, boys, I'm going to run for a third term!"

Soon, a political button said: "Washington *wouldn't*, Grant *couldn't*, Roosevelt *shouldn't*".

Speculation about a run for a third term started even before FDR's second inaugural. The President seemed to enjoy all the talk. Questions about his intentions for 1940 were a regular feature of his weekly Oval Office press conferences. Like when a *New York Times* reporter popped the question, to which Roosevelt replied with a comment about the weather. The writer doubled down, "Mr. President, would you tell us now if you would accept a third term?" FDR said, "Put on a dunce cap and go stand in the corner."[2]

The Road to 22

Any discussion about the idea of congressional term limits must include a look at what Congress—yes, Congress—did when it came to limiting how long presidents could stay in office. Call it irony or even hypocrisy; the record is clear. But the far-from-self-aware institution that functions a few blocks away from the White House seems to perpetually miss the obvious—not to mention the point.

Most, if not all the arguments opponents of efforts to limit how many terms members of Congress can serve applied to the debate by the 80th Congress more than 75 years ago. But such arguments fall on mostly deaf ears on Capitol Hill. After all, how many politicians are capable of rising to the level of statesmanship required to govern themselves? Asking any institution to police, much less limit, itself carries with it an inherent conflict of interest.

Very few political leaders in history have voluntarily let go of the reigns and trappings of power. We'd like to think there would be many examples of humble selflessness, but that's not the case. Sure, someone will usually say, "George Washington did it voluntarily." Yes, he did. But are there many leaders like him in Washington these days?

Name one.

When it became politically possible for Congress to put constrictions on the goose they would never permit on the gander, the House of Representatives and the United States Senate seized the moment with relish. And what they did remains the constitutional law of the land today.

It's the Twenty-Second Amendment to the Constitution of the United States.

Wouldn't

The framers of our Constitution agonized over the issue of creating the office of president. They feared the idea of one-man rule, having fought a war to get out from under it. They didn't want an American king but saw value in having a national leader. And with George Washington in the room, there was no doubt who that leader—at least the first one—would be. Some liked the idea of making the presidency a lifetime appointment. John Adams even proposed he should be addressed as, "His Elective Majesty," but those ideas didn't get much traction.

Good thing.

Though the issue of term limits was debated for a while in

Philadelphia in 1787—largely because the concept had been part of the outgoing Articles of Confederation—the final draft of the Constitution was silent on the subject. The issue was thought to be one of those things that would be played out in the future for good or ill. And it was just a few years later when George Washington opted not to run a third time and retired to Mount Vernon in 1797.

How he left office—as were so many things Washington did—started a tradition. There is little doubt he could have served in the office for the rest of his life, but he shared his countrymen's fears about central government becoming too powerful. Though it was nowhere chiseled in stone, Washington's decision set a precedent that managed to temper and frustrate political egos for the next 150 years.

Couldn't

But because it was not an actual matter of law, a few of Washington's successors seemed at least to ponder the possibility of a presidential hat trick. The most notable was another general who became president—Ulysses S. Grant. After his reelection to the White House in 1872, many Republican leaders wanted to see the popular war hero ignore the precedent set by the first military commander to serve as president and declare his intentions to run for a third term. Grant was clearly interested but didn't want to have to fight for it. He shut such talk down and was succeeded by Rutherford B. Hayes.

Hayes barely won the most contested and controversial election up to that time and pledged not to run for reelection—a promise he kept. That set the stage for supporters of the still wildly popular Grant to try to orchestrate a comeback.

In fact, former President Grant decided to allow them and went to the 1880 Republican National Convention as the front-runner for the nomination. He led after more than thirty ballots, but eventually lost to James A. Garfield.[3]

On election night in 1904, Teddy Roosevelt, when winning his own term after serving the lion's share of the assassinated William McKinley's, pledged to keep the two-term tradition alive and issued a statement that he would not run again in 1908. But like General Grant, he couldn't resist the siren call to run again in 1912, only to lose to Woodrow Wilson, a man who—had his health been better—might very well have tried for number three himself. And a few years later, Calvin Coolidge—someone who might very well have succeeded in breaking Washington's tradition—shut down all speculation with his terse declaration, "I do not choose to run for President in 1928."

Shouldn't, But...

The last years of the 1930s were turbulent on the world stage. A gathering storm of war clouds hovered over Europe and Asia, and people began to talk about things like preparedness. Franklin Roosevelt watched what was happening across the seas but always with one eye on domestic politics. There is a sense among historians that he "never had any intention of retiring after two terms if he could present a third term as a matter of duty." To run again would be challenging, but not impossible "to such a master politician."[4] And as the world moved toward war, he clearly believed himself to be indispensable. So he let it be known that if he were to be drafted and nominated, he would serve another four years.

The Democrats drafted and renominated him on July 17, 1940.

Wendell Wilkie was the Republican nominee, and he said about FDR's bid for an unprecedented third term, "if one man is indispensable, then none of us is free." But in the end, the power of the incumbency during a time of unprecedented international crisis proved too much for the opposition to overcome. FDR was elected that November. Then, four years later, he was elected *again*.

But he only lived to serve 82 days of that unprecedented fourth term.

Time for Change

The year following the end of World War II proved to be a turbulent and transitional one in America. While the world calmed down, the country heated up. The military downsizing and mass homecoming put great pressure on the labor market. Unions that had pretty much sat out the war as part of their patriotic duty became active and aggressive. There were more than 5,000 strikes in 1946 involving nearly 5 million workers. The war had accomplished the kind of recovery that the New Deal never came close to bringing about, and those who had survived the ravages of war were understandably hungry for their piece of prosperity pie.

On the political front, November's midterm elections saw Republican majorities sweeping into both the House and Senate. The time was ripe for change, which for many meant the dismantling of parts of FDR's program and getting America back to the kind of fiscal responsibility and limited government that existed back when Republicans ran the show.

One of the interesting ironies in American political history is that the move toward the implementation of presidential term limits in the wake of Franklin Roosevelt's long tenure in the White House was, at least in part, instigated by the work of the man FDR trounced in the 1932 election—former President Herbert Hoover.

Job one for the new Congress was creating a group to study ways to streamline government services, and Mr. Hoover was appointed the chairman. He had already been invited back to the White House by President Truman for the first time since his unceremonious exit in 1933. Truman felt the former president's banishment by FDR was mean-spirited and at least a measure of rehabilitation was long overdue. By the time Hoover began his work on the commission that would soon bear his name (the Hoover Commission), Truman had made his peace with the idea of Republicans being more of a force than they had ever been throughout his own political career.

The Hoover Commission made several hundred recommendations to Congress and President Truman, including one dealing with the establishment of term limits for a president. Of course, Republicans had long championed the idea and were quite vocal about it in 1940 and 1944 when Roosevelt ran for and won unprecedented third and fourth terms, but they were the minority party.

Emboldened after their 1946 sweep, Republicans moved their initiative to the top of the heap where it was quickly drafted and approved. They sent what would eventually become the Twenty-Second Amendment to the Senate. In a few months, a polished version was sent to the states for ratification, a process that took a few years. It was finally added to the Constitution in February 1951.

> *No person shall be elected to the office of the President more than twice, and no person who has held the office of President, or acted as President, for more than two years of a term to which some other person was elected President shall be elected to the office of the President more than once. But this Article shall not apply to any person holding the office of President when this Article was proposed by the Congress, and shall not prevent any person who may be holding the office of President, or acting as President, during the term within which this Article becomes operative from holding the office of President or acting as President during the remainder of such term.*

Cynics look back on this as something crafted to be a political insult to the memory and legacy of Franklin Roosevelt. Of course, the politics of the prior fifteen years no doubt played into it, but there can be little doubt that had the president winning four terms been named Coolidge, Eisenhower, Reagan, or Theodore Roosevelt, the "other" party would have tried to do the same thing.

It was simply a good idea whose time had come.

Bear in mind that Congress was the driving force behind presidential term limits. How different would things have been if the issue of term limits for a president had to be decided by, well, a president? The inherent conflict of interest would be glaringly apparent. That's why the Framers of our constitution put the checks and balances in place between branches of government.

Self-interest is seldom in the public interest. But self-interest makes the world of politics go around, and human nature tells us that we have great difficulty choosing to do things that might undermine our ambitions.

If the country saw the benefits of limiting the terms of the executive, the need for such limits is even more important for the legislative branch that controls the "purse." The examples set by Washington and continued through to Roosevelt demonstrate the need to limit the time in service and provides a blueprint that should be adopted for the legislative branch of government.

What We Can Learn from Presidential Term Limits

The politics and processes that brought the Twenty-Second Amendment to pass in so many ways resemble what we're dealing with now when it comes to Congress. The motives and arguments made more than seven decades ago when the issue was the potential limiting of presidential terms transfer pretty well to our current discussion. When we codified what had been tradition since America began, we channeled our national inner George Washington, who said, "an elective monarchy is not why we fought the revolution." And up until Franklin Roosevelt's tenure, most Americans agreed with FDR's cousin, Theodore Roosevelt, who called the two-term presidential tradition "a wise custom."

FDR was reelected to a third and fourth term because of the power of the incumbency. Can there be any serious argument that Ronald Reagan would have lost a race for a third term if the Constitution didn't prohibit it? How about Dwight

Eisenhower, Barack Obama, or even Bill Clinton? The man from Little Rock would have been a better campaigner than Al Gore, who barely lost. And George H. W. Bush, Reagan's VP, won handily in 1988. Does anyone doubt that Obama would have been a stronger candidate than Hillary? My point is that incumbency is powerful. Theodore Roosevelt would have done better against William Jennings Bryan in 1908 than William Howard Taft did—though Taft won, which proves my point.

In the aftermath of World War II, America was recovering from a conflict instigated by leaders who had held too much power for far too long. Abuse of power by Hitler, Stalin and Tojo had blown up the world and killed millions. We were fearful—correctly, I might add—of unbridled executive power, something Franklin Roosevelt relished.

After all, on his first day in office, he sent a clear signal and set the tone for the next dozen years. Never one to let a crisis go to waste, he warned: "But in the event that the Congress shall fail to take one of these two courses, and in the event that the national emergency is still critical, I shall not evade the clear course of duty that will then confront me. I shall ask the Congress for the one remaining instrument to meet the crisis— broad Executive power to wage a war against the emergency, as great as the power that would be given to me if we were in fact invaded by a foreign foe." You might want to read those words again. They became the man's job description.

It was actually more than a warning—it was a *policy* and *prophecy*. The defining quality of Franklin D. Roosevelt was that he was the ultimate political animal. He thrived on politics. Today we might call him a political junkie. And like all such people, he thrived in the midst of chaos and looked for ways to leverage it for personal gain—in other words, power.

This is important to understand as we examine how and why the Twenty-Second Amendment came to be. Critics of this suggest it was some sort of political payback, vengeance in the form of law, on the part of disgruntled Republicans. However, though some did jump on the bandwagon for presidential term limits because they despised the political figure often angrily described as "that man in the White House," there weren't enough diehard FDR haters around actually to amend the U.S. Constitution. We need to look beyond petty animosities to understand what was happening then to help us better understand what we need to do now.

While the successful push for presidential term limits was undoubtedly, at least in part, an exercise in political backlash, it was, in fact, about much more. The accumulation of power marked Roosevelt's time in the White House—and the man was ruthless in its pursuit. One way he was able to pull this off was by creating a persistent counterfactual mythology about what was going on. The guy was a master of illusion and delusion. He was like a combination of Houdini and Machiavelli. He once remarked, "I am a juggler, and I never let my right hand know what my left hand is doing."

Probably the most effective and persistent myth is that FDR ended the Great Depression. But nothing could be further from the truth. He took office in March 1933, but eight years later, and after he had exercised that "broad executive power" he spoke of in his First Inaugural, Henry Morgenthau, FDR's Secretary of the Treasury, and the man who was closer to him personally and politically than anyone, said this in testimony before the House Ways and Means Committee:

> *We have tried spending money. We are spending more than we have ever spent before, and it does not work. And I have just one interest, and if I am wrong, somebody else can have my job. I want to see this country prosperous. I want to see people get a job. I want to see people get enough to eat. We have never made good on our promises...we have just as much unemployment as when we started...And enormous debt to boot!*[5]

Unemployment was actually higher than it had been during the darkest days of the Hoover administration. But somehow historians still to this day keep the myth alive.

So, whatever the backlash, it wasn't merely politics as usual. Roosevelt had demonstrated why no president should serve more than two terms. As the years rolled on, his forays into the realm of power run amok became more pronounced and dangerous. Of course, FDR's modern-era fans will point out that the times called for "broad executive power," but that's not quite right. Those dark days—through the Great Depression and World War II—called for action, but it didn't have to be unilateral and bypass the safeguards codified by the Founders and Framers. Roosevelt possessed a measure of vindictiveness surpassing that of Richard Nixon, and he used the government as his arsenal, specifically the IRS and FBI. And he was not a fan of the nation's highest judicial body, remarking: "We must save the Constitution from the Court and the Court from itself."

He was clearly suffering from what Calvin Coolidge described a year or so after leaving office, having opted not to run for reelection in 1928, an election he would have likely won handily. Coolidge said:

It is difficult for men in high office to avoid the malady of self-delusion. Worshippers always surround them. They are constantly, and for the most part sincerely, assured of their greatness. They live in an artificial atmosphere of adulation and exaltation, which sooner or later impairs their judgment. They are in grave danger of becoming careless and arrogant. A change in the Presidential office increases the chances of having wise and faithful public service after a moderate length of time.[6]

And the same can apply to members of Congress.

My point is that Roosevelt's lengthy tenure was a wake-up call to the fact that too much power corrupts. We need to understand what really happened in the late 1940s in order to effectively do what needs to be done today. Otherwise, myths, half-truths, and outright lies will guard the status quo and thwart the vital issue of term limits. We need people with a strong sense American history to serve in Congress. Otherwise, the nation's purse strings will be controlled by a conspiracy of the clueless.

Speaking of clueless, Representative Alexandria Ocasio-Cortez (D-NY) once remarked on MSNBC, during a discussion about congressional term limits: "When we look into our history, when our party was boldest—the time of the New Deal, the Great Society, the Civil Rights Act and so on—we had and carried super majorities in the House, in the Senate. We carried the presidency. They had to amend the Constitution of the United States to make sure Roosevelt did not get reelected."

What?

We've all heard electoral horror stories about the names of

dead people being used in voter fraud. But a presidential term limits amendment wasn't passed until 1947, and not ratified until February 1951. Franklin Delano Roosevelt died on April 12, 1945—do the math, AOC.

The story of the Twenty-Second Amendment is powerfully relevant to the current push for a similar one regarding service in the House and Senate. What I find fascinating about it is the fact that it is among the least discussed of any amendments to the Constitution. When it was debated in Congress in 1947, there was little debate, and it was hardly covered in newspapers around the country. What little discussion there was centered around a few key issues—and those same issues are part and parcel of today's debate relating to congressional term limits. Let's look at a couple of them.

The Indispensable Man

One of the primary reasons some members of the House and Senate hang around on Capitol Hill for so long is that they feel their continued presence is imperative. Congress needs them, they think. But is it more about needing Congress and all that it does for them? Politicians today too often view themselves like FDR did in 1940 and again in 1944—as indispensable.

During the ramp-up toward passage of the Twenty-Second Amendment in the House, a congressman from New York, Edwin Arthur Hall, expressed concern that "the natural love for power that men in high places often have is increased the longer they remain at the helm. They tend to shape the destiny of a whole people according to their single mind if allowed to go unchecked."[7] And invariably, as one senator put it, "when the time comes and the opportunity to continue themselves in office and power is presented, they always yield."[8]

Roosevelt's twelve years in office (that would have been sixteen years had he not died less than three months into his fourth term) saw the most significant expansion of presidential power in our nation's history. He created the modern presidency in his own image. Had he gone home to Hyde Park, New York at the end of his second term, much of that expansion would not have occurred—for example, those things he did with the world war as a cover. But he persuaded his party and then the American people that only he could guide the nation through those troubled times.

While the 1940 election gets the lion's share of historical attention in the debate about presidential term limits because it shattered the tradition of just two terms, which had been in place since George Washington's day, the election four years later is really the more troubling. That's the one that brought the "indispensable man" issue out into the open. Though he would lose that year to FDR, Republican nominee Thomas E. Dewey, the Governor of New York, spoke powerfully and eloquently about the matter. He said:

> Let us have no more of the pretense about indispensable men. There are no indispensable men. If our republic after 150 years of self-government is dependent upon the endless continuance of one man in office, then the hopes which animated the men who fought for the Declaration of Independence and the Constitution have come to nothing. The man who wants to be President for sixteen years is, indeed, indispensable. He is indispensable to Harry Hopkins, to Mme. Perkins, to Harold Ickes, he's indispensable to a host of other political job

holders... He's indispensable to those infamous machines in Chicago—in the Bronx—and all the others.[9]

Much has changed in America and the world since 1944, including an amendment to limit how long a president can serve. Still, Congress has more than its share of members who see themselves as indispensable as Roosevelt did. He was wrong then. And they are wrong now.

Term Limits and Democracy

Democrats who opposed presidential term limits in 1947 argued that they limited the people's rights. And Democrats who oppose congressional term limits do the same thing today. It's an old argument, one that has been around since the beginning of our republic. During the Senate debate about the proposed Twenty-Second Amendment, one member of that body put it this way: "I think our people are to be safely trusted with their own destiny. That is the spirit of democracy and its intent. We do not need to protect the American people with a prohibition against a President who they do not wish to elect, and if they wanted to elect him, have we the right to deny them the power?"[10]

The same thing is being said today about congressional term limits—that it is anti-democracy. But it's not. And how the Republicans responded to the argument in 1947 can help us counter it today. At the time, Wisconsin Senator Alexander Wiley said: "When we guarantee that no individual will occupy the Presidential office for more than two terms, we serve to encourage political leadership in other individuals. We assure a constant replacement of new blood into important positions in political parties."[11] He and his Republican colleagues correctly understood what those of us who support congressional term limits understand today—the Constitution was about democracy, but not without checks and balances in place. Presidential term limits were simply one more example of that concept. And congressional term limits will be yet another. We are not a pure democracy. The United States of America is a constitutional republic. As one House member put it: "Political apathy is a menace to democracy, and blind faith in a leader inevitably means an indifference to great issues and problems. Along with public apathy, there is a stifling of other leaders, so that the capacity for political leadership is weakened."[12]

Republicans knew that the longer someone stayed in office, the harder it was for that person to be removed. It is true for executive leaders, and the same is true for legislators. Sure, Republicans in 1947 were partly motivated by partisan concerns, but the bigger issue was that they shared something with the Framers—they saw power as something that needed to be tempered and limited. The presidency had become a much more powerful office than was originally intended. Similarly, the Congress, as it now functions, driven by career politicians, is a far cry from the citizen legislature it was intended and designed to be.

Age, Health, and Leadership

When we see images of leaders in Congress that clearly show them as not able to function as well as they did twenty years ago, it should remind us of the wisdom of limiting how long such people should be permitted to serve. Is the nation well served by men and women (in either political party) who would be too old to hold a job in the private sector? Frankly, the only people in their 80s who are still around in business are those who own their own companies. They can't be removed. It's the ultimate entitlement. And I think the reason so many members of Congress oppose term limits is because they see themselves the same way—they own the place. But they don't. We do—at least we're supposed to.

The Franklin Roosevelt story speaks to this issue powerfully. We now know that there was a massive cover-up about his deteriorating health when he ran for his fourth term in 1944. When his new running mate, Harry Truman, had lunch with him at the White House at the outset of that fall's campaign, he was horrified by how Roosevelt looked and how his hand shook when he tried to put cream in his coffee. The President had some severe health problems and was already living on borrowed time. And he was not only declining physically—his mind was not what it once was.

Yet, he ran. Americans elected him. He traveled to Yalta early the following year to shape the post-war world. He was so out of touch that Stalin played him like a violin. Could the coming Cold War have been avoided, or at least mitigated, had a younger and tougher man been negotiating with the Soviet dictator? I'm sure of it. But Roosevelt and his supporters saw him as "The Indispensable Man." Give me a break.

I love the poem with that title by Saxon White Kessinger. The gist of it is that though your ego may tell you "you're the best qualified man in the room," there really is no such thing as an indispensible man.[13]

As required reading, a copy should be sent to every member of Congress—the largest gathering of "the indispensables" in the nation.

CHAPTER FOUR

THE CULT OF CAREERISM

"Those who have been intoxicated with power... can never willingly abandon it. They may be distressed in the midst of all their power; but they will never look to anything but power for their relief."
—Edmund Burke

STORIES ABOUT THE FADING HEALTH OF LONG-TERM WASHINGTON POLITICIANS are popping up in the news more and more these days. Whether it's Senator Mitch McConnell freezing during a press conference and having to be led away, or the late Senator Diane Feinstein giving her daughter power-of-attorney over her personal affairs, too many political leaders seem to have held on to the reigns of their power far too long. Like an aging athlete who can no longer compete, politicians in their 80s and

90s are shells of their former selves. It's not that they're old. That's an honorable part of life. They don't know how to stop.

If there is no mechanism to stop them, the evidence is clear—they won't step down voluntarily. They're not capable of quitting. They won elections, and they intend to enjoy the fruits of victory. And like the late Muhammad Ali, they are determined to climb into the ring and answer the bell. It's sad when a sports hero does that. But it's more than sad when a politician does it. They put themselves and our political way of life at risk.

If congressional term limits were in place, you'd likely never see the image of an elderly legislator struggling to walk or find words. Very few people in their seventies would consider running for office for the first time. They know when it's time to head to the beach, golf course, or grandkids (not in that order, mind you).

Why do so many members of Congress stay in office so long? To find the answer, we need to circle back to the faith factor. And by that, I don't mean faith as a verb, as in to believe, but faith as a noun, as in a foundation of truth, as in "keep the faith." One of the key components of faith as truth is a recognition that we are prone to making bad choices.

Because human beings are fallen, we are easily tempted by power and money. Left to our own devices, we tend to make poor choices. And one of those choices is to cling to the things that feed our egos. The original sin was not eating an apple or any other fruit in the Garden of Eden. It was committed long before that—in heaven—when Lucifer's heart became filled with *pride*. And that sin remains the deadliest of the deadly and at the root of so many other forms of corruption. The annals of history are filled with examples of this. But the most powerful ones are found in Scripture.

Think of King Saul, who clearly let power and glory go to his head—and heart. He became consumed with pride, and when that was combined with insecurity and jealousy, he became a pathetic leader. The man who followed him was a better man—at first. But after he was long on the job, his pride and boredom led to terrible things. David took his eyes off the ball and ruined his life and that of much of his family. In fact, most people in the Bible we look back at as examples of faith had skeletons in their closets. They were sinners in need of redemption.

Very few people are immune to the temptations that accompany prolonged power. Sure, there was that guy Lucius Quinctius Cincinnatus, who answered his country's call to serve and lead more than 400 years before the birth of Christ. He left his farm to guide Rome through times of crisis and was given and exercised vast power, only to relinquish that power and return to his farm when the fiery ordeal was over. That's why George Washington is referred to as "The American Cincinnatus." He willingly gave his power back to the people and retired to Mount Vernon, leaving a powerful example to his political successors and all of us.

But do we have any such examples today? No. In fact, there is evidence that several presidents since FDR have pondered just how to get around that pesky Twenty-Second Amendment. Politicians seem to be like that gambler the singer Kenny Rogers told us about; they simply don't know when to walk away or when to run.

As leaders continue in power for prolonged periods of time and accumulate even more power, it's clear that they tend to become more isolated and less empathetic. In fact, the primary way leaders grow as they hold on to power is in their sense of entitlement. And somewhere along the way, those leaders tend to forget how they became powerful in the first place.

Scientific evidence supports the idea that feeling powerful can lead to increased dopamine levels in our brains. In other words, power can be intoxicating. This can manifest in many ways, from bad decision-making to narcissism and even cruelty. Though usually associated with pleasure, this dopamine reaction means people can be addicted to *power*. This can lead to a ruthless focus on winning and explain the behavior of tyrants throughout human history. Dacher Keltner, a professor of psychology at the University of California, Berkeley, has studied the neurochemistry of power in great detail. His experiments support what Lord Acton described as the corrupting potential of power. He cites four ways power can corrupt:

- Power leads to empathy deficits and diminished moral sentiments.
- Power leads to self-serving impulsivity.
- Power leads to incivility and disrespect.
- Power leads to narratives of exceptionalism.[1]

By the way, Keltner also believes that making people feel accountable is one way to mitigate the corrupting influence of power. Putting term limits in place would be a great place to start making members of Congress more accountable.

Political Careerism vs. Public Service

Political careerism is the polar opposite of public service.

Take the polls—most of them show that more than 80% of the populace support the idea of term limits for members of Congress. Who makes up the remaining 20%? Well, I'm sure they are those who have a vested interest in keeping the status quo alive and well. They are the ones who do politics as a *career*.

A great example of this is Speaker of the House Kevin McCarthy. Because of how things are done in Congress, he ran for that powerful office because it was basically his turn. He was next. He had climbed the ladder, and the Speakership was the next rung. Now, he is third in the line of succession to the presidency. But is that how leaders should be anointed, I mean chosen? Seniority should not be the criterion for choosing such critical roles. Does such a system lend itself to finding the best person for the job? Now, I have nothing against Mr. McCarthy and know he will give his best to the job, but is that the best for *us*?

In contrast to political careerism is the concept of public service by servant-leaders. Servant-leaders make the greater good a priority and the well-being of others the focus. More than 50 years ago, a man named Robert Greenleaf wrote an essay on the subject and went on to lead a movement. The terminology was important—putting servant before leader. This is not what we often see in politics, where leadership, with all its perks and protocol, is the main focus. Throughout my life, I've appreciated leadership books by John Maxwell, a man who has championed servant leadership.

Of course, the servant-leader idea really goes back to Jesus, who said: "You know that the rulers of the Gentiles lord it over them, and those who are great exercise authority over them. Yet it shall not be so among you; but whoever desires to become great among you, let him be your servant."[2]

Servant leaders emphasize character and put people first. They have compassion and are good listeners. They see themselves as stewards, not owners—as empathetic, not entitled. They don't regard themselves as part of the ruling class but as subservient to the people. If this doesn't sound like today's politics as usual, it's because it is not.

Citizen legislators fit the servant leader model much better than career politicians. This concept is a rich part of our heritage in America. There was a time when people left their farms and other enterprises and committed a certain amount of time (always limited) to public service, after which they returned to their lives. They were like citizen-soldiers being called up to do a specific job, but once that was over, they went home.

This approach would certainly mean more diverse representation with people from many walks of life—farmers, bankers, entrepreneurs, educators, even pastors. Maybe it would be better if Congress were not top-heavy with lawyers. Some should be there, but the lawyer-track to Congress has been overdone. We need more people with real-world experience. America wasn't designed to be governed by a political aristocracy, but it seems like it has been that way too much of the time.

Term limits and returning to the idea of citizen legislators are ideas whose time has come. The age of professional politicians needs to end, and servant leaders need to step up. If elected to Congress, I will leave a job that pays me several times more than the salary I'd be paid for service in the House of Representatives. It would be a sacrifice, but one that I'd be more than willing to make—for a specific period—to serve our nation and those who elect me. I would bring to that service the expertise from my years in business. I believe that experience would be helpful in so many ways. For example, when there are hearings before the Federal Trade Commission, like those recently, about ways to improve the automobile buying process, and government talks about how it can save us billions of dollars, we need people in Congress who can spot a stupid idea and push back.

As Congress regularly seems to be tasked with "helping" people in the real world, it would be helpful if some of those "real world" people were actually in Congress.

American Deacons

I have served as a deacon in our church, and to my mind, that role is a wonderful illustration of what it means to be a servant-leader. The word itself—deacon—comes from a Greek word (*diakonos*) and literally means "a waiter, servant; anyone who performs any service," and the root means "to kick up dust, as one running an errand."[3] Another word for deacon is "minister," which can also be a political term, as in prime minister. And though it is usually used in politics in reference to someone in charge—a leader—and the whole servant aspect seems to be missing, there is no escaping the fact that ministers (leaders) are to be (and see themselves as) servants. We need to return to the original idea—political leaders as public *servants*.

With the accent on servants.

I remember back when COVID and the restrictions it created were in full swing. Part of my responsibilities as a deacon at our church at Liberty Park involved reaching out to some of the senior church members. One was a wonderful lady named Mrs. Bruton. I called her on the telephone and asked about her needs. She told me she needed some basic grocery items, so my wife and I did some shopping for her.

Because of COVID, we left the groceries on her front porch and talked to her through the door. She kept talking, was clearly lonely, and obviously didn't want us to leave right away. Before we left, we asked if she had any other needs. She said that she loved to read but was running out of material because the public library was closed. We asked about her interests and returned a few days later with several books.

It was so simple—serving someone. Meeting needs. But first, asking the right questions.

I think members of Congress should be the political deacons in America. It shouldn't be about playing a role, image, or the perks of office; it should be about helping others, meeting needs, asking questions.

In other words, they should be servant-leaders.

In his excellent book, *Servant Leadership in Action: How You Can Achieve Great Relationships and Results*, Ken Blanchard says, "Servant leadership, like stewardship, assumes a commitment to serving the needs of others. It also emphasizes the use of openness rather than control." But do we see this from members of Congress?

It comes to this—too many politicians aspire to high office because they want to *be* something. Servant-leaders, on the other hand, seek such opportunities because they want to *do* something. Too many politicians seek office because they hunger for the limelight and power. Servant-leaders, however, want to find ways to help others get what they hunger for. Too many politicians want to be pampered and promoted. Servant-leaders are willing to suffer and make a quiet difference. They are the embodiment of the famous Ronald Reagan maxim: "There is no limit to what a man can do or where he can go if he doesn't mind who gets the credit."

And I see a very real connection between servant-leaders and the concept of citizen legislators. They tend to be sacrificial and selfless, having left much behind to answer the call of duty for a specific purpose and length of time. Can anyone really argue that a Congress made up of servant-leaders wouldn't be more responsive to the American people and effective when it comes to laws and policy?

John Maxwell says, "The heart of true leadership is putting your followers ahead of yourself. For that reason, the best leaders give up their rights. As you move up in leadership, your options and rights actually decrease. With each new responsibility you accept, the fewer options you have."[4] He is absolutely right, but this approach is largely absent from American politics and governing.

How Congressional Careerism Developed

Congress in the nineteenth century clearly reflected what the Framers of the Constitution had in mind. It was a legislative body populated by amateurs, not professionals—reflective of the concept of citizen legislators. Before 1900, each new Congress was made up significantly by freshmen—usually more than 50% of the members.[5]

The change from that kind of citizen legislature toward a body filled with professional politicians came about for several reasons. One had to do with changes in how elections operated throughout the country during its first century of existence. Back then, voters, more often than not, didn't have the benefit of the secret ballot or ways to vote for individual candidates.

Elections were controlled by political parties. In fact, those parties even printed color-coded ballots bearing the names of all the candidates. Often, a voter would have to walk in front of others to a ballot box with that party-produced slate in hand, something that did not lend itself to privacy or preference.

During the last decade of that century, however, state after state adopted something first known as "The Australian Ballot." The name came from the election reforms put in place in the land down under even before America's Civil War. We know this today as the *secret* ballot. And it brought about not-so-subtle changes in American politics. People no longer cast a single vote for a party slate but could vote for individual names—and secretly.

That was the moment when running for reelection became an exercise in blowing one's own horn. Members of Congress could advertise their legislative prowess and cite their accomplishments to attract loyal voters as they sought election term after term after term. They could talk about all the government pork their longevity could bring back home.

Then came the 1910 coup d'état against the czar-like Speaker of the House Joe Cannon, for whom the Old House Office Building was named in 1962 (the Cannon House Office Building). This paved the way for the emergence of the seniority system. And with that came more self-promotion ammunition for House members as they sought reelection. After all, why would voters want to bring in someone new when the incumbent had accumulated so much power via congressional tenure? That is an argument voters regularly find irresistible because the value of a congressional seat seems to increase every time an incumbent runs again and wins.

Professional seniority is a clear advantage when running against an amateur.

So, when you combine the human tendency to accumulate power and hold on to it as long as you can with the ability to promote yourself as someone who can deliver the goods by virtue of longevity, it takes a significant issue to motivate voters to elect your opposition. And even those legislators who start out thinking (and even pledging) to rotate back to civilian life after a few terms find it hard to resist the siren song of seniority-driven security and the trappings of office.

With term limits in place for those who run for and serve in Congress, careerism would simply not be a factor in how the institution does its business. Think about it this way: Those who would come to Congress via a process that set limits on how long they can serve could not and would not have as their goal to make a career out of politics, or at least in the sense of serving forever in Congress. They would go to Washington secure in the knowledge that they would be going home for sure in twelve years. This makes it likely that those running for office would be coming from some successful career, one worth returning to one day.

In addition, the idea that, as former members of Congress, they would be valuable to a business as a lobbyist with connections to those still serving in Congress would be moot because those other members would be rotating out of office as well. So someone term-limited out of office would need to be able to go back to a real job. One thing this does is to ensure those running for office have some expertise to bring to bear on their service in Washington.

We know this to be true when it comes to the presidency.

Long-term service in Congress is not a well-traveled road to the Oval Office. We tend to elect people to the highest office of the land who have actually run something, be it a business, or a state. In other words, executive experience. It is worth noting that only three people have been elected to the presidency after lengthy congressional careers. Two of those, Lyndon Johnson and Gerald Ford, got the job by accident.

The case of the third man—Joe Biden—provides a compelling argument *against* seniority and *for* term limits. If Mr. Biden had been term-limited out of office after serving two Senate terms back in 1985 and sent back to Delaware, does anyone believe he would be in the White House today?

Turning Back the Clock

The cult of careerism has turned Congress into something that barely resembles what it once was. It's time to make Congress function as originally intended—as a representative body of American citizens who step away from their private lives to serve the nation. These citizens would do so consistently with an end game in mind. The plan was always to return home to family and community, not to become permanent parts of some elite American political aristocracy. They were dedicated amateurs, not professional politicians. But lest the label of amateur imply a lesser skill set, I'd remind you that amateur athletes have inspired the world in the Olympics. They tend to be younger and more passionate than their professional counterparts. Congress would be a much more effective institution if those who served had the mindset of our citizen athletes representing us every four years in global competition.

The best way for democracy to function and flourish in our

constitutional republic is for the idea of rotation in office to become the status quo. Regular change must become our new constant. The Framers didn't put term limits in the Constitution in 1787 because they fully expected citizens to serve for brief periods in office and then return home to resume their real lives. The idea of politics becoming a career was off their radar. They did not anticipate the power of incumbency or how executive and legislative offices would morph into caricatures of their original design. As one Anti-Federalist wrote, rotation in office "would give opportunity to bring forward a greater number of men to serve their country, and would return those, who had served, to their state, and afford them the advantage of becoming better acquainted with the condition and politics of their constituents."

Term limits will reset the clock and recover the spirit of 1787.

When you think about it, the idea of more people having the chance to serve in Congress is much more democratic than the permanence we have now. The concept of amateur legislators over professional ones is much more about the people. And there is no objective evidence whatsoever that the "professionals" do a better job than everyday citizens would. To see it any other way is simply elitist. It is also wrong. In fact, it's clear that the way things are now doesn't produce effective legislators but rather careerists who are more interested in defending the status quo than in problem-solving. Their biggest problem is ensuring they hold on to the job as long as possible.

The more politics is professionalized, the further we get from the original idea of representative government. Instead of authentic political representation, citizens become clients, and members of Congress become the experts. The professionals see themselves as above the rest of us. They know what is best for the rest of us. But for representative government to work best, there must be a real connection between legislators and the people. George Mason wrote, "the requisites of actual representation are that the Representatives should sympathize with their constituents; should think as they think, and feel as they feel; and that for these purposes should even be residents among them." Another Anti-Federalist, Melancton Smith argued:

> *The idea that naturally suggests itself to our minds, when we speak of representatives is, that they resemble those they represent; they should be a true picture of the people; possess the knowledge of their circumstances and their wants; sympathize in all their distresses, and be disposed to seek their true interests. The knowledge necessary for the representatives of a free people...should also comprehend that kind of acquaintance with the common concerns and occupations of the people, which men of the middling class of life are in general much better competent to than those of a superior class.*[6]

There is no way that the cult of careerism fits that model. The Framers never envisioned nor countenanced an elitist system with constituents as clients and members of Congress as experts. Political professionalism is driven by ambition significantly at odds with the kind of representative model the Framers designed. If the idea of representation is to connect citizens to the government, careerism is a hindrance. We should be suspicious of it. As historian Daniel Boorstin argued,

"The representative of the people must be wary of becoming a professional politician. The more complex and gigantic our government, the more essential that the layman's point of view have eloquent voices." Indeed. Is the layman's voice being heard today? I think not. It's been drowned out by the big professional choir that performs on Capitol Hill. I like something else Boorstin said: "Democracy is government by amateurs. The survival of our society depends on the vitality of the amateur spirit in the United States today and tomorrow. We must find ways to help our representatives preserve this amateur spirit."

One way would be through term limits, as Senator Ted Cruz (R-TX) has argued:

Term limits are critical to fixing what's wrong with Washington, D.C. The Founding Fathers envisioned a government of citizen legislators who would serve for a few years and return home, not a government run by a small group of special interests and lifelong, permanently entrenched politicians who prey upon the brokenness of Washington to govern in a manner that is totally unaccountable to the American people. Terms limits bring about accountability that is long overdue, and I urge my colleagues to advance this amendment along to the states so that it may be quickly ratified and become a constitutional amendment.[7]

We Need a Lombardi Moment

The Green Bay Packers had blown a lead in the fourth quarter of the 1960 NFL Championship game and lost to the Philadelphia Eagles. So when the players reported for training the following July, they were ready to pick up where they left off and work toward a better outcome. They assumed they were in for some attenuating workouts. But they were wrong. Their coach, the legendary Vince Lombardi, called the players together and held up a football. They all stared at him and it for a moment. Then he said:

"Gentlemen, this is a football!"[8]

He told them to open their playbook to page one and took them on a journey through the fundamentals of the game. Before taking the practice field, they studied blocking, tackling, throwing, catching—the whole ballgame. Several months later, they beat the New York Giants 37-0 for the championship. And Lombardi and his team went on to win it five more times over the next seven years. He never lost another playoff game. That's why the coveted Super Bowl award is called the Vince Lombardi Trophy.

America needs a "this is a football" moment regarding how things are supposed to work in Washington. It's time for what Barack Obama described as "fundamentally transforming the United States of America," but not in the ways he meant. I'd put it this way: It's time to transform America by returning to the fundamentals that the Founders and Framers believed in.

Just as it worked that day when he gave his famous locker room speech, the fundamentals can elevate any team or organization to greatness. And it can do it with our nation too. We are far too politically enamored with the idea of the next new thing. But sometimes the best new thing is actually an old thing that has been forgotten or thought to be obsolete. Sadly, many Americans are clueless as to the fundamentals of our constitutional republic. They include popular sovereignty, federalism, the separation of powers, individual rights, and the rule of law.

But one that has been forgotten by many is limited government.

In our system, the government's power is limited, not absolute. Following the American Revolution, which was fought so we could be free from rule by a king, citizens were on guard against any hint of tyranny, especially an imperious national government. So, in the Constitution, we find limits on the state's power. The Framers desired free people and free markets. The Bill of Rights—particularly Amendments nine and ten—makes this clear. The rights of people do not have to be expressly written in the Constitution, and the delegated powers of the federal government are only to be performed if specifically mentioned in the Constitution. The Constitution further limits government intrusion into other areas of political life, like thought, expression, and association.

Limiting how long someone can serve in office is in the spirit of the Constitution and is, when you think about it, one of the most remarkable political developments in human history. That's not hyperbole. It only exists here in America, and that existence is always at risk. The American Founders were careful students of history. Thomas Jefferson noted that "history has informed us that bodies of men and individuals are susceptible of the spirit of tyranny." Patrick Henry regarded history as a "lamp of experience." To our Founders, it was the prism through which they saw and understood how individual liberty worked best under a form of government that was both representative and constitutionally limited.

The Founders and Framers were students of centuries of human history, and our founding documents reflect that. History taught them about the importance of the division of power and concepts like checks and balances. Such matters weren't invented in 1776; they were simply strengthened and made possible for the first time in large-scale way. The shots fired at Lexington and Concord paved the way for a new nation conceived in liberty and limited by law.

Anti-Government?

As a knee-jerk reaction, some people charge that those of us who support the idea of limited government are, in fact, anti-government. It's an easy "gotcha" for liberals, but as we say in Alabama, that dog won't hunt. We're not against the government. Not at all. We oppose the concentration of too much power and its potential for abuse. The men who crafted the Constitution were skeptics about the nature and use of power. They were hesitant to overly empower a federal government. And they saw the issue as a balancing act. On the one hand, the whole reason for the 1787 convention was to fix the Articles of Confederation, which were widely seen as weak and ineffectual. But on the other hand, they didn't want to break the blessings of liberty by creating a statist monster.

Limited government was baked into the Constitution to safeguard liberty since a government limited in power would be less able to exercise power in abusive or oppressive ways. In fact, to the men in that Philadelphia room, the principle of limited government was an even greater protection for liberty than were the freedoms later codified in the Bill of Rights. Interestingly, Madison didn't feel a Bill of Rights was necessary because the limited government provisions in the Constitution pretty much covered freedoms of all types. That's why the original document had to be almost immediately amended ten times, thanks to the passionate work of the Anti-Federalists.

It's clear from any reading of history that for our first 150 years, this country saw limited government as a constitutional no-brainer. But, as I discussed in the previous chapter, Franklin Roosevelt's New Deal was a political game changer. The role of the federal government in the lives of Americans grew exponentially—long a progressive and liberal dream. The Supreme Court pushed back and ruled much of it unconstitutional, which is why FDR hated the court and sought ways to dilute its power. But the government has been an expanding universe ever since. It wasn't until the age of Reagan that any real attempt was made to slow its growth.

And we've been fighting the good fight ever since.

What we mean by limited government is that it can't make laws and policies arbitrarily. Those in power can't just do as they please. The Constitution limits them. I believe that term limits for members of the House and Senate are completely in line with the thinking of the Framers and the history-changing document they created. And those men who labored so well during the summer of 1787, if given a do-over today, would make sure "rotation in office" was chiseled into constitutional stone.

I can almost hear Madison's apology from history.

Term limits would eliminate careerism and create a Congress populated with citizen legislators in keeping with its original intent and design. The legislators would represent the average American much more effectively and efficiently than any collection of professional politicians. Such a Congress would be a much better keeper of the taxpayer's purse. They'd be temporary stewards on behalf of all Americans.

Current and future members of Congress should pay serious attention to the fact that term limits in general have been approved almost every time they've been on the ballot somewhere in America. Polls regularly indicate overwhelming public support for the idea. In fact, the issue of term limits may be the most significant example of how tone-deaf the political aristocracy on Capitol Hill is. The American people want a steady influx of new people serving in our nation's most important offices. But the deck is constantly being stacked against that.

We need representatives who are not focused on the next election and who put their undivided attention on what they have been elected to do—serving the people. We need men and women in Congress who will fight the good fight for us, not chronically poised to fight another disadvantaged opponent in the next campaign.

We must remember and heed the wise voice of the elder statesman of the bunch that long-ago summer in Philadelphia. Benjamin Franklin knew a thing or two about a whole lot of things. He was the premier intellect in a room filled with brilliant minds. He knew the world of business. He knew the world of history. He knew the world of politics. In fact, he knew the world—period. Franklin contributed wise counsel to his colleagues in 1787 when he said: "In free governments, the rulers are the servants, and the people their superiors...For the former to return among the latter does not degrade, but promote them." He knew that when politicians had to face returning to real life and live under the policies they had enacted, they'd be better equipped to make decisions with long-term consequences in mind. He was, of course, right. Remember Ben's wise words the next time you hold a hundred-dollar bill in your hand.

Let's replace the cult of careerism with term limits and citizen legislators!

★ ★ ★

CHAPTER FIVE

DOWN ON K STREET

"Da man! You iz da man! How much $$ coming tomorrow? Did we get some more $$ in?"
—Jack Abramoff in an email to an aide

ALONG WITH LORD ACTON'S AXIOM ABOUT POWER, another nineteenth-century political quote provides a good segue to what this chapter is about. It's attributed to Otto von Bismarck, the first chancellor of the then-new nation, Germany, who is said to have remarked, "Laws are like sausages. It's better not to see them being made." Speaking of Germany, that's where we get the word describing the practice of buttonholing politicians and trying to get them to vote a certain way. The word is *louba*, from which we get one that's much more familiar—lobby. Around the time our country was struggling for independence, theatergoers in Britain often encountered people called "box-lobby loungers." They were people who didn't come to see the show but rather hung out in the lobby in order to chat with VIPs who walked by to and from their seats. A few decades later, the political use of the term began to be used—as in lobbying and lobby*ists*. And even during the days when the Continental Congress was in session, lobbying was present when legislators received a petition from someone representing concerned merchants who desired an end to the tax on molasses.

In our day and age, that proverbial lobby is where money and power converge.

Even though some lobbyists talk as if they support the idea of congressional term limits, they really hate the idea. They spend years developing personal relationships with politicians and use those relationships the way espionage professionals use assets and those in law enforcement use confidential informants.

I have a perspective from the business world. When running car dealerships, I managed big marketing budgets and had companies I regularly worked with—my "go-to" people. Getting to know them was a vital part of our working dynamic. So I get how relationships impact business—and even political— decisions. This is why a regular rotation for officeholders would keep things from becoming too familiar and inbred. The idea of having someone leave Congress and then having to start all over trying to cultivate someone new scares them silly. But in the final analysis that would be healthier for the American public.

Not all lobbying is bad, of course. Lobbyists can help provide vital expertise and perspectives to members of Congress on key issues. The late Senator Robert Byrd (D-WV), a politician who could be the poster-child for the need for term limits, said, "We could not adequately consider our workload without them." But there is no doubt that, no matter how good or noble a cause may be, part of the lobbying process involves finding ways to get someone to compromise. And compromise is one of the main stops along the road to corruption.

Then, there is the issue of what happens when members of Congress leave office and use the familiar revolving door to become lobbyists themselves. How can that process not be inherently corrupting? Elements of this revolving door are inevitable and a natural by-product of politics as usual. But it can also undermine the democratic process.

This comes back to the faith component of things. Because human beings are fallen and prone to sin, we are easily tempted by power and money. Left to our own devices, we will make poor choices. Think of King Saul, or even his successor King David. Power made them vulnerable to temptation and corruption.

When it comes to politics today, there is so much money involved that the possibility of corruption is always nearby. Take the case of Jack Abramoff, the former lobbyist who is the poster child for political corruption. His story can tell us a lot about what's wrong with the status quo and why democracy in America is threatened. Most Americans know at least a little about Abramoff's transgressions. He became the very image of the excesses that can surround influence peddling. They named a law after him, *Justice Against Corruption on K Street Act*—a.k.a., the JACK act.

Oh, and Kevin Spacey played him in the movie based on his story—*Casino Jack*.

Abramoff, like most working lobbyists in Washington,

"hated the idea that a congressman who I had bought with years of contributions would decide to retire. That meant I had to start all over again with a new member, losing all the control I bought with years of checks." That's pretty much the party line for lobbyists, though some try to pay lip service to the idea of supporting term limits. But the other thing he said may surprise you: *"One of the best ways to reduce lobbyist and special-interest control in Washington is to enact term limits for members of Congress. If you want to see pigs screeching at the trough, tell them they can't stay there forever. There's no trough as dangerous as the one in Washington. So let's clean up the corrupt mess. Let's enact term limits and restore control of our nation to the people."*[1]

The man who pioneered lobbying as we know it today was a former aide to President Franklin Roosevelt named Tommy Corcoran, better known by the moniker "Tommy the Cork." He began the "revolving door" and the idea of top officials moving toward big money with offices on K Street, a thoroughfare that became to lobbying what Wall Street was to financial markets. Corcoran turned lobbying into an art form and provided "the evolutionary bridge between the crass fixers of the past who bought and sold congressmen and today's slick lawyers who serve the public interest for a short time and for the sole purpose of cashing in later."[2]

Traffic continues to flow across that proverbial bridge.

Lobbyists and Professional Politicians

Lobbyists on Capitol Hill outnumber the number of members of Congress by more than twenty to one. And that's just those who are registered. Beyond this, there are many others who operate "unofficially" in the shadows of Washington.

Needless to say, the industry is powerful and influential. And that's the point. They have toolkits filled with assorted instruments useful for their work. And that work is simple. You see, lobbyists are hired to be persuaders. They represent clients and interests who seek favor on this or that matter before our elected representatives. And because so much money is involved, they can significantly impact policy.

Over the years, there have been attempts to reign in the lobbying industry, but the persuaders find ways to beat the system. It is no exaggeration to say that the influence of K Street can be found in virtually every piece of legislation considered by Congress. Lobbyists are sent to Washington for the express purpose of talking to our representatives and trying to get them to vote yay or nay on their issues. And they know how to use money toward that end. While few politicians actually stuff their own pockets with cash—the recent case of Robert Menendez (D-NJ) notwithstanding—few politicians are able to resist the lure of campaign donations, even if they come with implied strings attached.

After all, the main goal of members of Congress is to stay there.

Putting term limits in place would take the lion's share of a lobbyist's power away or at least seriously mitigate it. Term limits would be K Street's kryptonite. Without the undue and unfair—when compared to the average citizen—influence of lobbyists, members of Congress would be both free and responsible to do novel things—like voting their consciences. They would not have the undue stress of worrying about winning all those elections. That's right, term limits would provide stress relief for members of Congress and the American people.

The Perpetual Campaign

Members of Congress today are in permanent campaign mode. Fundraising is job one. So those who are supposed to be about the people's business tend to make *their* business a priority. And that business is the pursuit of money. I suppose that sounds cynical, but it's true nonetheless. As soon as one election cycle closes, the clock starts ticking for the next one. And every tick of that clock sounds like an old cash register—cha-ching! If you have any doubt about what I'm saying, I suggest you try to look at your representative's calendar. You'll see all sorts of evidence—morning, mid-day, and evening. It's what they do. It's what they must do to stay in power. And each election cycle requires more and more money. Frankly, inflation—when it comes to those fundraising needs—dwarfs what real Americans have ever experienced. We're talking exponential. And this permanent fundraising campaign should concern Americans.

It sure concerns me.

This permanent fundraising culture on Capitol Hill creates a powerful imbalance when it comes to political competition. How many people considering running for Congress spend two years raising money? The deck is stacked against an effective challenge to an incumbent even before a would-be opponent sits at the table. With term limits in place, there would be more "open seats" because incumbents would be required to rotate out. It makes sense that the race to fill such a seat would not cost nearly as much as trying to beat an entrenched incumbent who has been building a war chest for a living.

Professional politicians have turned campaigning into a lucrative industry, and lobbyists understand and know how to exploit this. Permanent campaigning has eroded the quality of our representative system of government. Members of Congress spend way too much time chasing cash for their coffers. Permanence has become a political ideology, turning government into a vehicle designed to make politicians popular and indispensable. And that takes time away from their real reason for existence. But there is little hope that this will change unless and until something forces it to.

Something like congressional term limits.

Of course, Congress is only one part of the problem, but it is, in many ways, the most vulnerable part of the governmental process because of its connection to the voters. This is especially true when it comes to the House of Representatives. The election cycle is short—two years. More than other institutions, it is impacted by the current culture of the permanent campaign.

The term permanent campaign became part of the political vocabulary during the days of the Carter administration.[3] It was code for the idea of using governance as a tool to build and maintain popular support. It was inherently about reelection. Though it didn't work out all that well for the man from Plains, Georgia, it became its own permanent campaign. And it has marked a major change in politics, where officeholders now campaign more than they legislate or govern.

The Founders and Framers would be as shocked about this today as they would to see people using a smartphone or watching Netflix. In fact, they thought campaigning for office was rather unseemly. They were not fans of popular electioneering. Image often becomes more important than issues when campaigning becomes more important than governing. We've come a long way in America from lengthy essays in our newspapers

(*The Federalist Papers*) to political sound bites and Tweets. And we're not the better for it.

The financial reality created by the permanent political campaign is tailor-made for exploitation by the lobbying industry. They have access to the kind of money it takes to fuel perpetual running for office. When Mick Mulvaney was a member of Congress before his work in President Trump's White House, he recalled, "We had a hierarchy in my office in Congress. If you're a lobbyist who never gave us money, I didn't talk to you. If you're a lobbyist who gave us money, I might talk to you." As the late Senator Robert Dole used to say: "Poor people don't make campaign contributions."

Mick Mulvaney's approach is still the norm on Capitol Hill.

There is a clear and indisputable link between lobbying and campaign donations. And even if a donation doesn't come directly from a lobbyist, a lobbyist is somewhere in the mix. During a CNBC documentary on the lobbying industry, Sheila Krumholz, the executive director of the Center for Responsive Politics, said: "The biggest corporations are all making PAC donations and even direct individual donations. So sending an army of lobbyists up to Capitol Hill to follow that donation is kind of, you know, the one-two punch. You first give the donation, and you next have your lobbyist pay a call."

Various interest groups can connect with members of Congress in many ways, but lobbying particular representatives and making campaign donations is the road most traveled. And money is the most valuable tool in fending off serious challenges to an officeholder's incumbency. Would-be opponents start in the hole, and most find it hard to get any traction. They face deficits in things like name recognition, image, and an inferior platform. These problems are compounded by the fact that the typical incumbent can outspend them exponentially. Most challengers simply can't raise the kind of money it takes to beat a permanent campaign politician. This fact alone keeps so many great people from service in Congress.

How to Get Rich in Washington

Term limits would loosen the grip of lobbyists. They would ensure each representative would serve for a constitutionally limited time. Those who desired to make a difference and be favorably remembered as public servants would be less likely to be in permanent campaign mode. Instead, they would be more involved in governing and building a legacy. Term limits in Congress would not remove all the power from lobbyists, but it would effectively reduce some of the more questionable aspects of it. That's why lobbyists don't want congressional term limits.

It would put most of them out of a job.

It is no secret that K Street functions like the Wall Street of professional politics. All you have to do is, as the saying from the days of Watergate goes, "follow the money." Lobbying is where the real money is made, and term limits would certainly change that—at least somewhat. There will always, of course, be well-funded and highly paid agents of influence in and around Washington, but term limits would temper things. They would also make a post-legislative lobbying career less attractive to members of Congress rotating out of office. That would make them much more likely to return home, which the Framers intended to happen.

A report in *The Washington Post* noted that in 2021, the lobbying industry raked in more than $3.7 billion, and 3,700 new companies and organizations hired professional arm twisters to work on members of Congress. One researcher declared, "Every aspect of the economy the past couple of years has been in full-blown crisis mode, so everyone got involved in lobbying."[4] And the situation has undoubtedly continued to get worse. That same expert added, "I think it's likely there are some people who came to Washington a couple of years ago and have stuck around, or industries that realized the benefits they could accrue by having an active presence in Washington."

Understandably, lobbying as it is now practiced and funded in Washington makes those of us who live and work outside the Beltway uncomfortable. The whole process needs to be more transparent. Lobbying takes place below the radar and in the political shadows. Lobbyists deal in the currency of information. They also deal in the currency of, well, currency. They are influential with members of Congress. They also influence elections.

Did you know that some lobbyists actually get involved in writing bills? It's true. Just have a serious conversation with a lobbyist sometime. It won't take long for you to learn that they help create the nuts and bolts of public policy. They help members of Congress by contributing ideas and even doing some of the writing. There's a whole lot of copying and pasting on Capitol Hill. Part of this is due to the extraordinary time demands on our representatives, but some of it is just an easy surrender or abdication of the responsibility to think through complex issues. Sometimes, lobbyists function as ad hoc staff members, particularly when the twenty-something aides lack expertise or life experience for more complex matters.

If you talk to lobbyists, you'll quickly learn that a good

part of what they do is help their allies with the nitty-gritty of developing and passing policy. Some of that involves generating ideas, and some of that involves actually writing the legislation. Congressional offices rarely have the time or resources to develop their own policies—certainly not on complex issues like derivatives. Most Americans would be surprised—even shocked—to learn that our elected representatives don't create or invent original legislation. The detailed work is done by staff members and the lobbyists who inform and influence them. Business, industries, and organizations hire those lobbyists to sell their ideas to members of Congress.

Those same outside groups also fund the campaigns of the representatives they need to pass legislation favorable to them and their causes. It's a win-win for them and legislators. Not so much for the rest of us. The simple fact is that significant amounts of legislation don't originate on Capitol Hill. Congress does not come up with every legislative idea; more often than not, the process begins with a particular interest group. Lobbyists are well compensated by those groups to persuade legislators to go along. It's a tried-and-true system, but more tried than true. When you elect a representative, you are not actually—for the most part—voting for someone who will work at his or her desk for long hours carefully crafting the language of legislation. That's a myth. Our representatives regularly vote for or against legislation already written for them.

Now, I want to be clear. I am not anti-lobbying. Lobbyists can and do serve a vital function. No member of Congress can know everything about everything. Having access to expert advice is very important. But the system as it now exists is out of control and needs fundamental reform. The best way to change Washington's culture regarding "influencers" would be to implement congressional term limits.

Term limits would return lobbying to something more helpful and benign.

★ ★ ★

CHAPTER SIX

SENIORITY, INCUMBENCY, AND AMBITION

"As long as the seniority system is in place, politicians will hold on to office as long as possible. Term limits would be a huge step toward a meritocracy on Capitol Hill."
—U.S. Senator Tommy Tuberville (R-AL)

SENIORITY CAN BE A GOOD THING, especially when it is tied directly to experience or merit. I mean, you wouldn't make a cadet graduating from West Point a two-star general, no matter how good his grades or important the family connections. No religious denomination would make someone newly ordained a bishop. But the idea that simply because someone is older (even much older) and has held a job for a long time doesn't mean he or she is the best person for the job. Tenure and competence don't always go hand in hand.

In the middle of the nineteenth century, a very young minister took London by storm. But the phenomenon had an unusual catalyst. When he was just nineteen years old, Charles Haddon Spurgeon shared a message at a conference of ministers. He quickly found himself on the receiving end of some sarcasm from an older minister who was offended by Spurgeon's youth and perceived audacity. The critic said that it was a pity such young boys didn't follow Scripture and "tarry at Jericho" until their beards were grown—a reference to a verse in the book of II Samuel. It was quite the gotcha moment.

Young Spurgeon asked the moderator for a chance to reply. He later wrote: "I reminded the audience that those who were bidden to tarry at Jericho were not boys, but full-grown men, whose beards had been shaved off by their enemies as the greatest indignity they could be made to suffer, and who were, therefore, ashamed to return home until their beards had grown again." What Spurgeon did not know was that his critic had earlier disgraced his calling and was forced to spend some time away from his ministry. Take that. And as providence would have it, one man who witnessed the exchange was a deacon at a once famous and formidable church in London. The deacon was impressed with Spurgeon and invited him to speak at his church. The rest, as they say, is history.[1]

Sometimes, the best person for the job is not the one with the seniority.

You'll likely never find another institution or enterprise where seniority counts as much as the United States Congress.

Length of service is the lifeblood that flows through its corridors and guides all aspects of the legislative process. The seniority system—though not specifically codified anywhere—has, as is the case with all intractable processes, been around for a long time. It probably began with the Senate as they early on sought ways to limit the power of a vice president who served as the president of the Senate as called for by the U.S. Constitution. Senators understandably preferred to be led by one of their own, the president pro tempore.

Around the time of the War with Mexico (1846-1848), a system of standing committees was put in place by the president pro tempore, followed soon thereafter by a similar system installed in the House of Representatives by the Speaker of the House. Those leaders became more and more powerful through the ability to appoint people to chair and serve on committees. Over time, the system has evolved and changed, but it remains one driven by seniority. And the longer someone stays in Congress, the more powerful they become, something that *always* gives an incumbent an edge over a would-be rookie in an election.

Fans of the seniority system make several arguments beyond the idea that it values experience. They insist it also helps create harmony among legislators. You see, by having such a system in place, hurt feelings can be avoided when someone clearly more qualified is passed over. But of course, most successful private enterprises would rather make appointments on the basis of merit because that brings a greater chance of success. How novel.

Implementing term limits for members of Congress would neutralize the seniority system. Seniority doesn't guarantee competence. Experience doesn't always mean expertise.

And the ability to win election after election doesn't qualify someone to chair a committee.

One seldom-noticed flaw with the seniority system is how it actually keeps highly qualified citizens from even contemplating a run for Congress. Take, for example, the case of someone who has served well in another government post, maybe as part of the executive branch. Let's say someone has served as Secretary of State or the U.S. Ambassador to the United Nations. Whatever the political perspective, such a person would certainly have expertise and insight that could serve the Congress well. One could envision such a resume worthy of chairing a Foreign Relations committee. But the seniority system insists that a person must start on the bottom rung of the ladder. Why would such an experienced person run for the House or Senate?

It seems like the seniority system and its so-called bias toward experience actually inhibits people with stellar experience from aspiring to serve in Congress, no matter how patriotic they are and how profound their desire to serve their country. Think about it: there have even been former U.S. presidents who left office young enough to be of service to the nation, like Winston Churchill did after he was voted out of office in 1945. He went back to the House of Commons and became the voice of the loyal opposition. Whatever you think of the politics and policies of leaders like Jimmy Carter, Gerald Ford, either George Bush, Bill Clinton, or Barack Obama, just because they left the White House, a case can be made that at least one of them might have had a great second act. Some have actually excelled in public service after being exiled from Washington—Herbert Hoover and Jimmy Carter come to mind. How many great Americans could have been voices in Congress as opposed to in the political wilderness?

The congressional seniority system seems to attach very little significance to a person's knowledge base. The main thing is length of service. But term limits would change that. How much time one served in office would be a non-factor—knowledge and hands-on experience in a particular field or enterprise would be the primary considerations. And by the way, removing a particularly powerful and long-term committee leader is almost impossible under the seniority system, even if the leader is clearly too old and has lost touch. That would never be the case in a Congress tempered by term limits.

The congressional seniority system has been a legislative straitjacket far too long. As Senator Tuberville says, "The seniority system will always be a roadblock to term limits. Politicians will cling to power because the longer they do, the more powerful they become."

How many times have you heard arguments like this: "Well, I don't really like the guy's record in office, but I'd sure hate to see our district (or state) lose all his seniority and committee assignments." This is a common sentiment when it comes time to vote again for a member of Congress. And the self-serving political cycle continues spinning around and out of control. Organic reform of the archaic seniority system would have game-changing impact on congressional term limits.

Incumbency

One of the most common arguments against congressional term limits usually goes like this: "We don't need term limits. We already have them. They're called elections."

But as *tweet-worthy*—even reasonable—as that might sound, the reality is much different. The longer a member of Congress serves, the more unlikely it is that barring some major misstep, that person will be voted out of office. Why?

The power of *incumbency*.

Incumbency and careerism are flip sides of the same political coin. The electoral advantages inherent in incumbency are self-evident, yet regularly ignored, minimized, or outright dismissed in the congressional term-limit debate. A would-be legislator running against an entrenched Washington politico starts out in the hole. The person already in office has a decided, almost insurmountable, advantage. And any discussion of term limits without dealing with this important factor is meaningless.

An incumbent has access to many perks that come in handy when the next election rolls around. They have resources at their disposal that outsiders don't. With a large staff on the public payroll they can provide things to constituents a mere office seeker cannot. This fact alone inhibits many otherwise talented and public service-oriented local citizens from risking an expensive and likely unsuccessful challenge.

My passion for congressional term limits and the concept of citizen legislators is part of an overall vision of getting back to where our country started and what it was meant to be. Service in Congress was decidedly temporary, something people passed through rather than made a permanent home. Take the case of a man named George Robertson, who represented Kentucky in the House of Representatives when James Monroe was in the White House. Robertson served, got reelected, then went home. Years later, while writing his autobiography, he said:

> *I had been elected for a third term, the elections being the year before the commencement of the term. But, on my return home after the close of my second term, I resigned my third term. I was pleased with political life, and my prospects were encouraging. Had I been affluent, or without a family, I would have preferred to continue in public life. But, poor, and having a growing family, I felt a paramount and sacred obligation to give up my political prospects, and devote myself to my profession and my wife and children.*[2]

His story was common in those days. That was when Congress was an arena for debate and decision. The spoken word was king. Arguments were thought-through and articulated with passion. Nothing like ours—the age of the sound bite or slogan. Over time, Congress grew into the professional organization we know today. By the mid-twentieth century, incumbents dominated the congressional landscape, and the House and Senate were no longer some kind of temporary stop on the road to somewhere else, but rather a career itself complete with its own culture and trappings. In other words, *careerism*. Someone with ambition could make long-term service in Congress their life's work. And the seniority system facilitated that.

Ambition

Ambition can be a very good thing. Through it people have achieved great things, fulfilled amazing dreams, and made better lives for themselves and their loved ones. From entrepreneurs to athletes to scientists and artists, people driven by ambition have changed the world. In fact, nothing great is ever accomplished without it.

But do ambition and politics always mix well? After all, ambition should never be unbridled. It needs to be tempered by other concerns—particularly morals and ethics. There is a world of difference between a young Ted Williams having the ambition to be the greatest baseball hitter who ever lived and the distorted ambitions of the likes of Hitler or Al Capone.

Unchecked political ambition is a root cause of tyranny. Recall Lord Acton's axiom about power and corruption. While few would aspire to an office without a measure of ambition, the desire for fame and prestige can become problematic. The founders understood this. It's why they were so careful about things like checks and balances. And that's really what the issue of term limits is about—another manifestation of checks and balances.

In a system designed for citizens—the People—to run things, great care must be taken to ensure the ambition of some doesn't devolve into something sinister and destructive. In our representative republic, we put people in charge who will—at least theoretically—govern on our behalf. We call them leaders, but they are really supposed to be our servants. The idea of a ruling class should be repugnant to us.

Ideally, we need people who love America to seek elective office to serve the nation. But it doesn't take a rocket scientist to figure out that such a system can be exploited by people with selfish ambitions. So, it is always a balancing act. An ambition to become a member of Congress is not a bad thing. Why apply for a job you don't want? But it goes back to the idea of faith mentioned throughout this book. We need to understand our common flawed humanity.

And we need some ground rules.

I referred elsewhere in this book to my service as a deacon. Well, there's another great analogy for politics that comes from the church. When the Apostle Paul wrote to his young protégé, Timothy, he said, "If a man desires the position of a bishop, he desires a good thing."[3] The Greek word used for "desire" is often translated elsewhere as "covet" or "lust." In other words, it's a reference to a very strong desire—like a passionate ambition. It's not wrong to want something very much. The bigger issues have to do with why you want it and what you want to accomplish. Pastors can serve, or they can lord it over others. But only one is right.

By the way, I Timothy 3:1-7 is a great read for *anyone* who is ambitious to lead *anything*.

When it comes to politics, how someone behaves and plays the game will be directly related to his or her ambition. This means the tendency to behave in a way calculated to improve the chances of getting power and holding on to it. Thus, the need to keep an eye on ambition and to, at times, take steps to keep it in check. To my mind, this is what the whole discussion of term limits is all about—preventing unchecked ambition.

As I've noted, the founders understood this. They understood human nature. They were much more self-aware than many leaders today. These days we seem to be surrounded by too many who are overly optimistic about human nature and human potential as if history doesn't inform us otherwise. Madison dealt head on with this issue in *The Federalist Papers* when he wrote: "Ambition must be made to counteract ambition." The Father of the Constitution also said this in Federalist No. 51:

> *It may be a reflection on human nature that such devices should be necessary to control the abuses of government. But what is government itself but the greatest of all reflections on human nature? If men were angels, no government would be necessary. If angels were to govern, neither external nor internal controls on government would be necessary. In framing a government which is to be administered by men over men, the great difficulty lies in this: You must first enable the government to control the governed; and in the next place oblige it to control itself.*

What he and the other Framers did was to, in effect, use human nature as a weapon against human nature. They didn't ignore or deny humanity's sinful propensity, they harnessed it. They used our common core problem to keep that common core problem in check. They correctly understood that unbridled ambition has always been, and will always be, the enemy of freedom. And when unchecked passion for power, fame, and wealth run amok, it is always at the expense of true liberty. That's why Madison said, "All men having power ought to be distrusted to a certain degree." This was the thinking behind everything related to the separation of powers.

It is also the thinking behind the push for congressional term limits.

A healthy democratic process requires ambition, of course. But at the same time we need to understand and better inform people about what is appropriate and what is not. And this goes back, as so many issues do, to cultivating a collective moral sense. That is not something government can do; it must happen in the private sector. John Adams understood this when he wrote: "We have no government armed with power capable of contending with human passions unbridled by morality and religion. Avarice, ambition, revenge, or gallantry would break the strongest cords of our Constitution as a whale goes through a net. Our Constitution was made for a religious and moral people. It is wholly inadequate to the government of any other."[4]

Apparently, our second President was a prophet.

The ambition to lead was something the Founders and Framers understood, but they knew it needed to be controlled, because it can and does have a dark side. History teaches us this. The world is filled with morally "flexible" people who pursue their goals with no regard for others. Machiavelli is alive and well in American political culture. Rolfe Peterson, a political science professor at Susquehanna University, says, "Politics is at times such a dark place with manipulation, calculation, and conflict inherent in the activity. We should not be surprised that people who exhibit negative social traits may be drawn to politics and other people might be repelled."[5]

Implementing term limits—yeah, it's important.

Meritocracy, Not Seniority

There's a place in America for considerations based on seniority. It can be a way to keep top performers on the job and can be a stabilizing influence on a business or organization. But it is usually one factor among many used to determine things like promotions in the private sector. Most companies prefer a merit-based approach—who is the best person to do the job? In other words, a meritocracy. After all, most human beings in their 80s don't function like they did in their 40s—or even

60s. It's a fact of life. Maybe it's sad, but it's the way things are.

Seniority is always about the status quo. When it comes to business, the status quo is the loser lane. Without change, you get left in the dust of your competitors. Former U.S. Army Chief of Staff Eric Shinseki said, "If you dislike change, you're going to dislike irrelevance even more."[6] The problem is that when it comes to the seniority system in Congress and representatives who have long since ceased to be relevant, they don't see themselves that way. They assume that if they exist and persist, they are important, even indispensable. I like what Peter Drucker said: "It's easier for companies to come up with new ideas than to let go of old ones." As an entrepreneurial businessman, I know that to be true. Progress and innovation go hand in hand, and defending the status quo usually gets in the way.

It's been said that the best way to kill an enterprise is when seven words are in charge: "We've never done it that way before." An organization driven by people who rise through the ranks will tend to be sluggish. Sometimes the best people for a job are a few rungs down the ladder. A culture of seniority is driven by a "wait your turn" approach. The criterion is not "who's best"—it's "who's next." But the world is full of examples of how putting the wrong person in a role simply because it was their turn led to decline and even disaster. Even a casual survey of American companies will show the superiority of meritocracy over seniority.

When an organization emphasizes merit, competition increases, followed closely by productivity. People are advanced because of what they've done and can do. It's a more accountable way of doing things. It empowers employees. Whereas a seniority system tends to kill motivation. Having a system in place that values and recognizes high-performing employees can ensure those productive people are acknowledged for their efforts. Seniority-based promotions tend to push the high performers out the door and toward better opportunities with companies that "get it."

How many politicians in Washington today got where they are because they simply stuck around? I agree with Alabama Senator Tommy Tuberville when he says, "The seniority system in the Senate and House creates careerism. We need a merit-based Congress, not one driven by tenure."

Would an 80-year-old man be running for a second term in the White House if he didn't feel it was his turn and was determined to keep it his turn as long as possible? It seems myopic and selfish. Congressional term limits would neutralize the seniority system for all practical purposes and move the House and Senate toward a system based on other concerns—like who would be the best person for a particular committee chairmanship. To my mind, this is a no-brainer. But those who breathe the rarified air inside the Beltway want to guard the status quo against all enemies and at all costs.

A meritocracy-driven system levels the playing field, something Congress needs. As things are now, the longer someone stays in office, the more things lean toward them. Wouldn't it be better for the nation if we found ways to choose the best people for positions rather than having to settle for leaders simply because they've lived many more years than the rest of us? I believe in respecting our elders, but when they reach the age when you have to ask them for the car keys (always tough but necessary), why do we insist on letting them keep the keys to political power?

Meritocracy leads to a fairer system overall. The results speak for themselves. Expectations are more precise. What business owner hasn't had to deal with a problem employee who has stayed too long in a particular role? It's like a toothache—nothing changes until it is pulled, or you have a root canal. Well, term limits would give Congress the root canal it has needed for a long time. Painful? Yes. But without it, our prolonged national political toothache will worsen.

With a Congress reflective of the results of regular rotation, the newcomer and the veteran would be treated just the same, which is a better way to serve the American people. Instead, we're stuck with the "it's my turn" politics of seniority. And when it comes to the consideration of congressional term limits, the issue is a double-edged sword. On the one hand, the American people want them, as poll after poll, year after year indicates. Yet, when it comes down to voting for particular representatives, it's evident that someone who, by virtue of longevity in office, has brought the bacon home is hard to vote against. Pork barrel politics tends to win the day.

However, without a seniority system that becomes an electoral advantage, particular elections would become more competitive. An incumbent's record would be at issue, not power accumulated over time. This is one of the primary reasons no serious discussion about term limits occurs in the House or Senate. Seniority increases a representative's power and ability to deliver pork-barrel products back home. That won't change until term limits are in place. And because seniority rules now, expecting Congress to do anything about term limits willingly is a pipe dream.

Twelve years in Congress should be enough time to accomplish anything worthwhile—who needs 30 years?

Eliminating the seniority rules in the House and Senate, something that would be the fruit of term limits, would end the establishment of personal power centers in Congress. It would also, of course, significantly weaken the power of lobbyists. Incumbents would no longer have incredible advantages over challengers at election time. The potential corruption of so much money would be largely neutralized in the process.

Eliminating the seniority system through term limits would go a long way toward preventing the gridlock we often see on Capitol Hill. Members of Congress could choose their committees in coordination with their peers. It was never the intent of the Framers to see power in Congress shift toward specific leadership positions. And that power shift has made Congress less effective in representing the American people. I think limiting the power of leaders would be a good thing and restore that power to individual representatives—which was the original constitutional model. And since Congress is about as likely to fix itself as a crook hoping to find a police officer, real change must be forced on them by the people.

The Incumbency Edge

It is simply a matter of fact that incumbents enter any election campaign cycle with a decided advantage. They are nearly always a good bet to win. Only in cases with unique facts—like some scandal, political upheaval, or a sitting member of Congress has just done a lousy job—enters the mix do we see incumbents booted out of office. It's quite rare. Too rare, frankly.

The decision for a citizen in any district or state to challenge a sitting member of Congress is always difficult. Someone has to put their regular life on hold and try to figure out how to raise enough money—the current thinking is that it takes about a million dollars to run for a seat in the House of Representatives. Incumbents have little problem raising what they need for obvious reasons. This fact alone is enough to scare many great candidates who would make excellent representatives away.

One political science professor, Gary Jacobson from the University of California-San Diego, says: "The electoral value of incumbency lies not only in what it provides to the incumbent but also in how it affects the thinking of potential opponents and their potential supporters. Many incumbents win easily by wide margins because they face inexperienced, sometimes reluctant, challengers who lack the financial and organizational backing to mount a serious campaign for Congress."[7]

His analysis is spot on.

The best candidates seem to be drawn to elections for open seats, as is the case when someone in office chooses to retire. Those elections, all-too-rare events, in my opinion, tend to be harder fought and more competitive than the specter of a long-shot candidate running against a well-heeled incumbent with a big war chest. But that's how incumbents like it. And the opposition party's response is token.

Take the case of Gerry Connolly, who represents Virginia's Eleventh Congressional District. A long-time Northern Virginia politician, Connolly routinely trounces would-be challengers. In fact, in 2016, the Republicans couldn't find anyone to run against the guy. He won with nearly 90% of the vote—the remainder belonging to several write-in candidates. This kind of thing happens more than you might think because of the incumbency edge.

The Key to Real Reform

Our Constitution detailed a system of government that could be effective as a servant of the American people. But politicians long ago began to move us away from basic principles of political fairness and toward a culture that empowers individual politicians and helps them "serve" perpetually. The establishment of congressional term limits, which has been the case for the executive branch for more than seven decades, is the premier political reform needed in America today. It will solve so many problems and ensure our national return to the fundamentals of our constitutional republic. Term limits would neutralize the advantages of incumbency, create healthy turnover in the House and Senate, make for more responsive representatives, scale down the amounts of money involved in campaigns, and curtail the government's wasteful spending. Who can argue with these benefits?

Professional politicians, that's who—those who thrive on the cult of careerism on Capitol Hill. Term limits will be a bulwark against elected officials' undue accumulation of too much power. And they will give the voters in each district more—and better—choices at the ballot box. More than 80% of Americans support the idea. Can you think of any other issue in our nation where the people so overwhelmingly want something but that our elected representatives simply ignore?

As William Natbony writes, congressional incumbency "is a paradigm of careerism, combining power, stature, and influence with lavish benefits: a high salary; unparalleled business connections; limited working days; spectacular working conditions; periodic taxpayer-funded fact-finding trips; a sizable staff (that could include family and friends); exceptional medical, dental, and retirement benefits; weakened insider trading rules; taxpayer-funded legal expense; the ability to moonlight at other jobs; free flights back and forth to the lawmaker's home state; a family death gratuity; and free parking."[8] And if you've driven in Washington, D.C., that last one is really cool.

I think of an old George Gershwin song from the 1930s and 1940s when I read about the perks of incumbency. I hear these lines:

> *Nice work if you can get it,*
> *And if you get it,*
> *Won't you tell me how?*[9]

★ ★ ★
CHAPTER SEVEN

PENDULUM POLITICS—WHAT CAN WE LEARN?

"Bureaucracy defends the status quo long past the time when the quo has lost its status."
—Laurence J. Peter

THE VISION THE FOUNDERS AND FRAMERS HAD WHEN IT CAME TO THE HOUSE OF REPRESENTATIVES was in line with what we might refer to these days as an entrepreneurial one. They were builders who created a new way of government out of their dreams. And ever since, there has been a struggle between that entrepreneurial spirit and one best described as a spirit of bureaucracy. What we have now is a bureaucratic Congress.

What we need is an entrepreneurial Congress.

Term limits will help that happen.

Think about it this way. Most Americans who understand reality know that for our economy to be successful and vibrant requires people willing to take risks and pursue their dreams. In other words, entrepreneurs. And for these risk-takers to pave the way for a larger national prosperity, it is vital that they be encouraged in their efforts and that no unnecessary obstacles be placed in their way. The more the government seeks to control things via tax policy and assorted regulations, the less likely the chances for an entrepreneur to be successful. And we should always bear in mind that these visionaries drive the economy. As it goes with them, so it goes with the rest of us.

The government doesn't produce anything. In fact, it funds its own enterprises by taking resources away from the very enterprises that make America prosperous. This is done with a bureaucratic mindset. To the bureaucrat, the government knows best. It is an omniscient force that always seeks to become omnipresent and ultimately omnipotent—all-powerful. The founders knew this was the default principle of governing based on human nature. It becomes all about power—acquiring it and hanging on to it as long as possible. What else could explain the absurd idea of leaders who clearly suffer from the effects of age and illness resisting all efforts to get them to step aside?

Simply stated, bureaucracy undermines entrepreneurialism. Members of any bureaucratic fiefdom despise things like innovation. It threatens their very existence. The results don't matter. All that is important is staying in control. And bureaucracy is everywhere—even in the United States Congress. And

I can't think of a better way to keep the power of bureaucracy in check and its anti-prosperity practices at bay than to have more entrepreneurs serving in Congress. A shift, via term limits, away from a bureaucratic Congress to one dominated by entrepreneurialism will obviate now common images on Capitol Hill like a way-too-old-and-ill senator unable to communicate.

Term limits will help create a congressional culture of *innovation*. We need legislators who know how to think outside the box, not people who spend most of the time building and protecting their own boxes. We need legislators who are willing to change Congress. Risk takers. Rule changers. When bureaucrats dominate Congress, the tendency is to perpetuate the status quo. In other words, staying in Congress is the number one priority.

We must never forget the entrepreneurial dynamics present and pervasive at the beginning of our republic. The Founders and Framers managed to temper their natural human self-interest and created something that, in a real sense, must be rediscovered and carried forth by each new generation. Our national history teaches us we must guard against human nature's default tendencies, even in Congress. Without political vigilance, the creeping influence of bureaucracy will dominate. Like some kind of creepy law of political gravity, there is a constant pulling coming from the bureaucratic direction. Left alone, it will draw American politics—our way of life, for that matter—ever downward toward diminished liberty and expanded government control and intervention. Liberty will, therefore, always be at risk.

Jefferson was right: "Eternal vigilance *is* the price of liberty."

Since the end of the Second World War, there have been a few moments when the entrepreneurial approach used by the Founders and Framers broke through the crusty topsoil of bureaucratic government and into the political light of day. And this was always driven by a new burst of energy in the conservative movement. Growing throughout the 1950s, conservative thinking gave birth to Barry Goldwater's run for the presidency in 1964. Sure, he was soundly defeated by President Lyndon Johnson, but seeds were planted at that moment. They would grow into something quite profound.

In the beginning was the word.

There have been a few moments in history when a speech propelled someone onto the national stage. Back in 1858, a little-known and often defeated politician from Illinois named Abraham Lincoln was invited to speak in New York. He worked long and hard on the speech, and in the weeks before, he rode five different trains east. The venue was supposed to be Plymouth Church in Brooklyn, pastored by the most famous preacher in the country—Henry Ward Beecher. But when Lincoln got to New York, he learned the venue had been moved to the Cooper Union in Manhattan.

He realized that he needed to change some of his speech in consideration of a less religious and more political gathering. In the audience on February 27, 1860, were political bigwigs and leading figures in the city and state. Also there were the editors of the *New York Times*, *New York Evening Post*, and the *New York Tribune*. He spoke for about 90 minutes. And the rest, as they say, is *history*.

That's what happened in October 1964.

The Goldwater campaign of 1964 has been called

everything from a "fiasco" to a "glorious disaster." Barry Goldwater had, in 1960, asked conservatives to "grow up." They did, and Barry was nominated four years later. But they faced forces of history, sympathy (in the wake of the Kennedy assassination), not to mention the personality and methods of Lyndon Johnson.

The cause was doomed, but like a bright star gleaming against the backdrop of a dark sky, someone who would eventually shape history stepped onto America's political stage at that moment. And it all began with a speech—some still call it *The Speech*.

Ronald Wilson Reagan's journey from Hollywood to Washington included a pivotal transitional period when he came into the homes of millions of Americans each week as the popular host of GE Theater, a program that beat *I Love Lucy* in the ratings. He leveraged that role and his celebrity into a speaking career, where he spoke out on the issues of the day—from the virtues of limited government to the evils of communism.

By the early 1960s, Reagan had established himself as an eloquent spokesman for the fledgling conservative movement, warning audiences about enemies abroad and within. He was making as much as $10,000 per speech—a hefty sum 60 years ago.

When Goldwater ran in '64, Reagan became co-chair of his California campaign, giving him more opportunities to speak out. One such event was a $1,000 per plate fundraiser at the Coconut Grove in LA, hosted by a wealthy car dealer. After hearing him that night, a group of donors came up with the idea of a national broadcast featuring Reagan's speech. They committed the funds to pay for the airtime.

Reagan agreed—but some of the Goldwater people were, shall we say, less than enthusiastic. In fact, some of Barry's closest advisors were fiercely opposed to the idea. They wanted to run a program showing Goldwater hanging out with Eisenhower in Gettysburg.

As Reagan recalled:

> *A few days before the speech, Senator Goldwater himself called me and mentioned canceling the address. His people told him that I talked about Social Security and he'd been getting kicked all over the place on the issue. I explained to him that I'd been making the speech all over the state and nobody had ever said anything. His people apparently wanted to repeat some show of former president Eisenhower and him strolling around fields at Ike's farm outside Gettysburg. I said, 'Barry, I can't just turn the time over to you, because it's not mine to give. A private group bought this time.' Well, he said, 'I haven't seen the speech or heard it, let me call you back.' So he got a copy of the sound track and listened to it. I'm told that when he heard it, he said, 'Well, what the hell's wrong with that?*

In the speech (called at the time *A Rendezvous With Destiny*—now *A Time for Choosing*), Mr. Reagan talked about the hot-button issues of the time, from Vietnam to the welfare state to taxes and the federal budget. The speech did not change the outcome of the election, of course. But it did make an impact—short- and long-term. First, it led to a last-minute frenetic flow of donations to the nearly bankrupt Goldwater campaign. It also "electrified" the nation. I've included the text of The Speech in the back of this book. It remains powerful and relevant.

For years, people talked about how The Speech impacted them. But no one was influenced by its success more than the speaker himself:

> *The night that the tape of the speech was to air on NBC, Nancy and I went over to another couple's home to watch it. Everyone thought I'd done well, but still you don't always know about these things. The phone rang about midnight. It was a call from Washington, D.C., where it was three A.M. One of Barry's staff called to tell me that the switchboard was still lit up from the calls pledging money to his campaign. I then slept peacefully. The speech raised $8 million and soon changed my entire life.*[1]

Ronald Reagan's presidential election led directly to a struggle between entrepreneurial and bureaucratic approaches to government. It was also a great moment for the U.S. Constitution. It is still referred to as the Reagan Revolution, and policies for tax-rate cutting, deregulation, and other things to encourage growth in the private sector were put into place. For the first time in modern American history, those who were passionate about conservative principles had national executive power. The problem was the conservatives didn't have overwhelming *legislative* power.

It took yet another revolution to make that happen.

In the years immediately following the Reagan years, the presidency of his vice president and heir apparent notwithstanding, that always-present struggle between entrepreneurs and bureaucrats saw the pendulum flow away from Reagan's ideas. By the time of Bill Clinton's election in 1992, much of the conservative agenda had been dismantled. The bureaucrats were taking over again, like weeds returning to a garden.

I think the attempt to implement government-run health care led by Hillary Clinton, an unelected activist who seemed to embody the bureaucratic vision, scared conservatives out of their stupor. It was then that Republican leaders decided to push back in a dramatic and ultimately effective way. They worked to take power back for the kinds of conservative principles Reagan talked about and worked hard to implement. Their plan was nothing short of a revolutionary attempt to overthrow the legislative bureaucrats and usher in a new group of legislative entrepreneurs. They crafted a pro-Constitution agenda and presented it to the people.

The Contract with America.

The Republican Revolution of 1994

What happened in 1994 with the Contract with America had its roots, of course, in the Reagan Revolution of the 1980s. Many younger members of Congress saw what had happened with the executive branch and had difficulty reconciling it with what they saw all around them on Capitol Hill. Republicans had been the minority for so long it was almost as if they had what some described as a minority *mindset*. The game as they knew it had been played the same way for so long, they—like a hostage resigning to make the best of captivity—decided the best way to get along was to go along.

After all, the last time the GOP had control of both the House and Senate was back when Harry Truman was president.

And that lasted just two years. Before that, the last time they ran all of Congress was when the stock market crashed, ushering in the Great Depression. Republicans were transcendent for a total of two years in the past 60 years. And that was very frustrating to a group of conservatives calling themselves the Conservative Opportunity Society. They began meeting together during Reagan's first term to develop a strategy to accomplish nothing less than the fundamental transformation of the House of Representatives and how it did its business.

They also had a vision for Republicans to become the majority party on Capitol Hill. They took the battle from the back benches to the front lines of American political discourse, demonstrating a tremendous flair for innovation and the use of futuristic technology.

The ultimate fruit of their efforts became the Contract with America.

So, on September 27, 1994, just six weeks before Americans would go to the polls in that year's mid-term elections, House Minority Leader Newt Gingrich (R-GA) met and stood on the steps of the U.S. Capitol in Washington with more than 300 congressional candidates to sign a pledge with voters across the country that promised to enact ten specific pieces of legislation during their first hundred days in office.

That hundred-day benchmark had been the gold standard for presidential activity since Franklin Roosevelt's sweeping New Deal bills during the spring of 1933, but it had never been tried or even promised before when it came to legislators. These candidates had, in effect, turned most local elections into a national referendum on all things Washington. Gingrich said, "A campaign *promise* is one thing, a signed *contract* is quite another."

Of course, Gingrich and all the others on those storied steps were mocked by the Democrats and in the media. Critics called it a Contract *on* America and assured their political base that it would not be victorious. But they underestimated both the vision and determination of its proponents and the ever-present political appetite of the American people for serious reform in Washington. The GOP took control of the House and Senate, picked up twelve governorships, and took control of twenty state legislatures that the Democrats had previously controlled. The Contract with America revitalized the Republican Party, captivated the American public, and nationalized the mid-term elections as never before. Gingrich later said of the Contract, "there is no comparable document in our 200-year history."

It was the ultimate game-changer.

And when the 104th Congress began its work on January 3, 1995, the clock started ticking immediately as critics and cynics watched to see if it had been just political smoke and mirrors. Over the next hundred days, Republicans worked feverishly to keep their promises. They did. Even the liberal *New York Times* had to acknowledge its significance with front-page language like, "Perhaps not since the start of the New Deal, to which many of the programs now under attack can trace their origins, has Congress moved with such speed on so many fronts."

The Contract was a promise to vote on ten key reforms. It was designed to draw broad public support and had a common-sense vibe. People got it. The reforms involved an assortment of initiatives relating to how the House did its business—the People's business—on the budget, taxation, and even welfare reform.

The Contract with America also included term limits.

During an address on the floor of the House, as the

Contract was being presented to the voters, Gingrich described the ten reforms it contained. The tenth and final one was, as he described, "Congressional Term Limits. Let us replace career politicians with citizen legislators. After all, politics should not be a full-time job."

Indeed.

But good old point number ten would turn out to be a bridge too far for many of those full-time politicos—the good old boys inside the Beltway. Although the previous nine parts of the Contract were quickly passed, the term-limits plank was defeated. It was unique because it called for a constitutional amendment, and that required the approval of two-thirds of the House, not a simple majority. The hope was to set a twelve-year limit on congressional service—two terms in the Senate and six terms in the House.

The best chance at term limits up to that point in our history—and ever since, for that matter—needed 290 votes to pass but only received 227. Interestingly, 38 Democrats voted in favor of it, but 40 Republicans, inexplicably, voted nay. In the immediate aftermath of the vote, one member of the House said: "The arrogance of this place is showing tonight—the arrogance of people who say, 'I'm indispensable. You say voters can get rid of you, but you have a bigger war chest, and higher name identification than anyone else in your district. Voters want to get rid of you, that's what their saying."[2]

One Democrat, who was clearly out of step with the rest of America, expressed that arrogance this way: "Sometimes the American people are wrong. This is one of those times." Really? If so, Americans continue to be "wrong" all these years later as poll after poll on the subject of term limits shows vast popular support for the idea. Could it be that the political "professionals" have been wrong all along?

I think so.

One reason for the failure of term limits to pass in the House, even though the other nine pledges made in the Contract with America did pass, was that not all Republicans were on board. As noted, forty GOP members balked at the idea. Significantly, thirty of them had been in Congress for quite a long time. Do the math.

Henry Hyde (R-IL) was the chairman of the House Judiciary Committee at the time, and he spoke passionately against term limits when the issue went to the floor. Hyde first came to Congress in 1974 and quickly made his presence known. He had a powerful speaking voice and a sharp tongue. His speeches tended to be erudite and attention-grabbing. Hyde, and the other Republicans who joined him in what in hindsight can only be seen as a betrayal of their GOP colleagues and the people who had swept them to a majority in the House due to the Contract didn't relish the idea of having to support something that would undercut their political situations.

Hyde pulled no punches in his speech, calling term limits "the dumbing down of democracy."[3] He added, "In times of crisis, we need people of experience." In other words, the "indispensable man" argument. He was the poster child for a seniority system that rewarded longevity. Hyde would be elected to Congress fifteen times.

The fact that so many Republicans voted against term limits was a political slap in the face of the voters who had been mobilized by the Contract with America, because the term-limits plank was among the most popular of all its promises. It was also further evidence that political professionals were—and are—inherently reluctant to act and vote against their own political careers. It's basic human nature, and it has been part of the American political fabric from the beginning.

Back in 1784, there were term limits when we had the Continental Congress. Members were required to rotate, as one member of the ancestral body noted: "Representatives ought to return home...By remaining at the seat of government, they would acquire the habits of the place, which might differ from those of their constituents." But when the time came to actually enforce the rule, all hell broke loose. Some incumbents pitched such a fit that the rule was ultimately shelved. James Monroe, our future fifth president, was there and later reflected: "I never saw more indecent conduct in any assembly before."[4]

A Political Bridge Too Far

In retrospect, what happened two decades ago was a teachable moment. Because fundamental human nature tends to trump even the best angelic impulses, changing something contrary to it is an uphill climb at best, and a bridge too far at worst. Pardon the mixed metaphor, but you get my point. Pressure brought to bear by the ballot box, such as was the case in 1994, is not enough. Because, at the end of the day, there will always be members of Congress who ignore the express wishes of the people and act out of anything but enlightened self-interest.

Term limits would curb human nature, but human nature resists those curbs—it's a classic catch-22. Though nine of the Contract with America promises were translated into legislative reality in the House, the tenth one—term limits for legislators—was not. The Contract represented a paradigm shift in American politics, but it fell short. The Republicans did amazing work during the first hundred days in 1995, but the one piece of the puzzle that could have made the most lasting difference was missing. Franklin Roosevelt had invented big government in his first hundred days; Republicans pushed back with relish then. It was an achievement of historic proportion.

They told the truth, and American voters embraced it.

Interestingly, Franklin Roosevelt's first hundred days created the time frame as a benchmark for political success. But FDR never told voters any specifics about what he would do. Just vague platitudes. When then-Governor Roosevelt ran against the beleaguered incumbent President Herbert Hoover in 1932, he attacked the Republican's "extravagant government spending." That's right, the man who would take federal spending to a whole new level of extravagance, sounded like a Reagan conservative as he made his case to the voters. He attacked President Hoover as "the greatest spender in history." And during a speech in Iowa in September 1932, he gave potential voters this gem of political chutzpah:

> *I accuse the present administration of being the greatest spending administration in peace times in all our history. It is an administration that has piled bureau on bureau, commission on commission, and has failed to anticipate the dire needs and the reduced earning power of the people. Bureaus and bureaucrats, commissions and commissioners have been retained at the expense of the taxpayer.*[5]

He seemed determined to prove true something the Sage of Baltimore, H. L. Mencken, said at the time: "Every election is a sort of advance auction sale of stolen goods."[6] Seen through the prism of what FDR actually did as president, it's hard not to conclude the guy had a serious problem with the truth. In Pittsburgh that year, he gave a major speech on the economy and suggested he wanted to explain federal spending by comparing it to a family's budget.

> The first and most important and necessitous step in balancing our federal budget is to reduce expense. The truth is that our banks are financing these great deficits and that the burden is absorbing their resources. All this is highly undesirable and wholly unnecessary. It arises from one cause only, and that is the unbalanced budget and the continued failure of this administration to take effective steps to balance it.[7]

Franklin Roosevelt was elected to the presidency on a promise to balance the federal budget. "I ask you very simply," he said often that year, "to assign me the task of reducing the annual operating expenses of your national government." The voters swallowed this hook, line, and sinker. And once in power, he did the opposite. Later, candidly, he asked one of his aides how to reconcile his extravagant spending with what he had said in that campaign speech. "Deny you were ever in Pittsburgh," the aide replied.

Roosevelt was a political chameleon, as with so many professional politicians. His thinking aligned with the old Groucho Marx wisecrack: "Those are my principles. If you don't like them, I have others!" My point is that FDR's fabled hundred days had never been understood by or voted for by everyday Americans. He did almost the opposite of his pledge to get to the White House.

But the Republicans in 1994 told Americans precisely what they would do if elected. It was quite a novel moment in our nation's political history when you think about it. Those ten promises were simply stated and clear enough to be grasped by everyone. With one voice, more than 350 candidates for Congress—a mix of incumbents and first-timers—said, "We are going to propose and enact these ten things." And they delivered—proposing all ten and enacting nine of them.

What made term limits the exception? That's easy to answer. The term limits promise was the only one with any possible way of threatening their political future. There is a good measure of the exercise in self-preservation surrounding the term-limits issue—and this cannot be overstated. Even a casual reading of history shows how intoxicating power can be. Related to that is the fact that people with access to power tend to, at least at times, place their own interests over those of their constituents. It's an issue as old as the Bible. Self-interest in the lives of people in power lends itself to self-serving political practices.

It is also clear from history that this has been less of a problem in the United States than in other nations—then and now—but we have been far from immune or exempt. Put simply, accumulated power can and does lead to abuse. This is, of course, at the heart of the idea of term limits as a necessary reform on Capitol Hill.

Americans are discouraged about the state of politics today. A recent Pew Research Center survey indicates approximately two-thirds of us "always or often feel exhausted when thinking about politics."[8] The report further indicates people see "no hope on the horizon." This is despite the fact that we have seen historically high levels of voter turnout in recent national elections. Also in the study is this tidbit, directly on point with our subject:

> *Majorities back age and term limits and eliminating the Electoral College. Reflecting the public's frustration with the federal government and political leaders, large shares of Americans support various changes to the political system, including for such long-standing proposals as establishing term limits for members of Congress and scrapping the Electoral College. Age limits—for both federal elected officials and members of the Supreme Court—draw broad support. But there is little appetite in the public for increasing the size of the U.S. House or modifying the allocation of Senate seats.*

Of course, a poll showing broad American support for term limits is routine—not to mention routinely ignored by those who make their careers inside the Beltway.

The almost complete success of the Contract with America taught us something significant. When the American people are frustrated and unhappy with political leaders, they are willing to listen to those who present serious alternatives. They are drawn to vision. And it's time to bring the vision for term limits in Congress to the people in a compelling way. From the ashes of its 1995 defeat in Congress and the Supreme Court ruling shortly after that (discussed in Chapter Nine), can rise a mighty political phoenix.

It will mobilize the people in every state to get this thing done finally.

CHAPTER EIGHT

LESSONS FROM MY WORLD

"I don't know who started the idea that a president must be a politician instead of a businessman. A politician can't run any other kind of business. So there is no reason why he can run the U.S. That's the biggest single business in the world."
—Will Rogers

As I mentioned earlier, I have spent my career working in and around the automotive industry, one of the most important areas of commerce in the history of our country. In fact, a powerful case can be made that cars made America what it is today—to us and the rest of the world. No invention impacted human life in the twentieth century more than the horseless carriage, as such vehicles were still referred to less than a century ago. Cars created the modern American economy, and they still drive it today. And when we think about this important economic engine, we must go back to a man who embodied the virtues and values of entrepreneurship and innovation.

Henry Ford.

The legendary American personality Will Rogers described Ford as a man who "changed the habits of more people than Caesar." One biographer called him "The tireless mechanic who put the world on wheels."[1] Even as a young boy growing up near Detroit, Michigan, during America's age of reconstruction after the Civil War, Henry showed an intense curiosity for how things worked. He would take clocks and watches apart so he could put them back together. By the time he was a teenager, he graduated to larger gadgets and began hanging out in his own small machine shop. In 1891, Ford began work as an engineer at the Edison Illuminating Company in Detroit. Thomas Edison, who would one day become his fast friend, was one of Henry's heroes.

Ford built his first internal combustion engine on his kitchen table in 1893 and his first car—the Quadricycle—in the early summer of 1896. By that time, he was the father of a little boy—Edsel. Henry founded the Detroit Automobile Company in 1899, but it went belly up in less than two years. His second company—the Henry Ford Company—didn't fare much better when Ford was fired by its board because he couldn't finish building even one automobile. That company actually survived and hired new leadership.

It eventually became the Cadillac Motor Company.

After raising $28,000 from several investors in 1903, Henry started yet another corporation—this one he called the Ford Motor Company. He burned through all but $300 of that money before selling his first car, but he was on his way. Announcing, "I will build a motor car for the great multitude," Ford went on to introduce his new brainchild, the Model T. He produced more than 15 million of the vehicles dubbed "Tin Lizzies" or "Flivver" over nearly 20 years, and with them, Henry Ford did nothing less than change the world. He also became famous and incredibly wealthy. He was the Elon Musk of his day.

Only much bigger.

The automotive industry fundamentally changed the world of business and commerce, and so many catchphrases found their way into everyday conversation. Some of those can be applied to this discussion about congressional term limits. Let me give you a few.

Upgrading the Model

The automotive industry regularly discontinues older models in favor of new ones marked by greater efficiency and evidence of innovation. Congress should learn from this. New ideas and fresh perspectives are the lifeblood of business. Why shouldn't it be the same in Congress?

Long before carpel tunnel syndrome existed, some people suffered from chauffeur's fracture. You've probably never heard the term because it goes back to how the first automobiles were started—by turning the crank. Then came the electric ignition. Aren't you glad you don't have to crank your car on a cold day—or a hot one, for that matter? If Congress ran the automotive industry, we all might still require treatment for chauffeur's fracture.

How about automatic transmissions, power steering, safety glass, seat belts, airbags, and GPS? The history of that industry is a study in innovation—making things better. And when a company opted for the status quo instead of the next new thing, it was usually the harbinger of bad things to come for their workers and shareholders. Henry Ford did not invent the automobile, nor was he the first to come up with the idea for the assembly line. He was an innovator. He looked for ways to make things better.

Until he didn't.

The story of Henry Ford is also a cautionary one about the dangers of age-driven stubbornness. You see, the man who innovated his way to unparalleled fame and fortune eventually fell victim to his own ego and desire for control. Sound familiar? He refused to move on from the Model T despite a shrinking market share and fierce competition, and he had to be dragged kicking and screaming into the future by his son and later his grandson.

There is something about growing old in the same job you've been doing for a long time. It seems to bring the worst out of people, which brings to mind politicos like Pelosi, McConnell, and Biden—hardly agents of innovation.

In the business world, innovators try to think like customers. They try to understand problems from their perspective. Lawmakers should try this sometime rather than just being smug and thinking Washington knows best.

Upgrades help a product stay working and relevant. Upgrades improve a product or service. Both of these things are needed on Capitol Hill. Change is the norm in the private sector. What's next? What's better? But when it comes to serving in Congress, those things are ignored. Sometimes I wonder if the members of Congress who have hung around way too long should have license plates on their cars that say: "Antique Legislator."

It's time for Congress to upgrade to a new model—term limits.

Tire Rotation

Even something as seemingly mundane as the regular rotation of the tires on your car can contain clues relating to the wisdom of congressional term limits. For example, we are encouraged to rotate them because it will help them last longer. But before you think this could be an argument for members of Congress to last longer in office, it is important to remember that when it comes to tires, we're talking about a project that has its own built-in term limit. They don't last forever; in fact, they are not designed for that. They simply work well during their time in use when they are in better balance via regular rotation.

Think of it this way—tire rotation is a metaphor for Congress as a whole, not just the individual members. Rotating the tires (members) of Congress is a great way to make it function much more efficiently. And it saves money in the long run. Does anyone really doubt that a term-limited House of Representatives (via member rotation) would be better equipped and motivated to watch the public's purse strings more closely? After all, pork-barrel politics drive reelection. Therefore, it follows that taking the chronic campaign mentality out of the equation would tend to reduce pet spending initiatives designed largely to enhance a member's next election.

If the principle of rotation is good enough for tires, crops, presidents, governors, and state legislators, why not for the big kahuna—Congress?

Every time Congress goes into crisis mode, as when a government shutdown is threatened, it's one more sign that what needs to happen is for America to put Capitol Hill in rotation mode. In ways that take hypocrisy to a whole new level, it is fashionable for members of Congress, particularly those on the left who are not fans of the highest court in the land, to call for the rotation (read: term limits) of Supreme Court justices. I will discuss this issue more in the next chapter but consider what Senator Bernie Sanders said: "We've got a terrible 5-4 majority conservative court right now. But I do believe constitutionally we have the power to rotate judges to other courts and that brings in new blood into the Supreme Court and a majority I hope that will understand that a woman has a right to control her own body and that corporations cannot run the United States of America." Nancy Pelosi agrees, saying there "certainly should be term limits." They need to be more self-aware. Not to mention retired and back where they came from.

If it's a good idea for the executive branch and a good idea for the judicial branch, why not go for the term-limit hat trick? That would certainly be good for America.

Recalls

In the automotive industry, when a defect is discovered, we issue recalls to fix the issue and prevent potentially bigger problems—even dangerous ones. Similarly, congressional term limits would serve as a regular and proactive recall to prevent potential problems related to prolonged tenure. After all, the longer anything is in service, the weaker it gets—that's basic physics. The Second Law of Thermodynamics tells us that, over time, order devolves into disorder—or *entropy*. Without exception. Like gravity, it is always at work.

A tree falls in the woods and then decays. Order to disorder.

And a nation built on individual freedom will gravitate toward tyranny over time. It's nature. It's human nature. A governing body starts out efficient and balanced and is only there to serve people and protect their rights, but the drift is always toward the disorder of dominating control of those very lives. And the longer Congress is dominated and led by entrenched incumbents, the more the drift toward national disorder.

As a conservative, I know it doesn't have to be that way. As Ronald Reagan said in that legendary 1964 speech, "You and I have a rendezvous with destiny. We'll preserve for our children this, the last best hope of man on earth, or we'll sentence them to take the last step into a thousand years of darkness." Sometimes, conservatives are accused of standing in the way of progress. But it's actually quite the opposite. We know that the natural progress of all things political is toward decline and disorder. We swim against that cultural stream. We are constantly fighting for the ultimate progress—freedom.

History is filled with examples of noble people and movements losing their way. Freedom is promised and embraced, only to give way to various manifestations of tyranny. And it is because of this we must have a constant and steady stream of fresh voices, seedlings for yet another eventual harvest of the kind of abundance only freedom can promise and deliver.

Congressional term limits would function as a built-in recall mechanism for the American people. Legislators would be working on a clock as most of their fellow citizens do. Their time would eventually run out, and they'd have to pack their things and head home—or somewhere else. We honor those who have served in our military. When we encounter a man in his 60s or 70s wearing a Navy ball cap, we are not tempted to ask: "On what ship do you serve, sir?" Instead, we usually say something like, "Thank you for your service." Past tense. He already did his bit for us. Job well done—emphasis on done. But when the more common way to thank a too-long-serving member of Congress is in a funeral eulogy, there must be a better alternative. There is—term limits.

The famous General Douglas MacArthur resisted retirement after World War II. He stayed in Asia and certainly played a significant role in rebuilding post-war Japan. He was 65 years old when he presided over the signing of the formal documents on surrender on the USS Missouri in Tokyo Bay on September 2, 1945. He could have returned home as a celebrated hero, but he stayed on. There was work to do, and he was sure that he was the only man to do it. He was indispensable. My point here is not to disparage a clearly great American—not at all. But in retrospect, had the man's ego, which had always been gigantic, outgrown his competence in his later years? Truman fired him in 1952—but the term used was "recall." And it was an unpopular decision by any measure at that time. Yet, history has not been kind to MacArthur, and Truman is now seen as courageous.

Could someone else have helped Japan in the postwar years? Sure. Could someone else have led our forces at the beginning of the Korean conflict? Of course. But those who serve in roles for so long that they begin to see themselves as indispensable are forever trying to convince us that they need to stay on, well, forever.

Competition

Another great parallel from my industry is the idea that the automotive industry thrives on competition. Manufacturers constantly seek to outdo the previous models to keep up with and surpass their competitors. Similarly, term limits would foster such an environment in Congress. Competition fuels creativity—the lifeblood of growth.

Without term limits, Congress is largely immune from the benefits of healthy competition. Incumbents are insulated and somewhat isolated—and many prefer it that way. The perks of office provide a barrier for them when the next election rolls around. The pool of potential election opponents is typically a small one. Term limits would change that dramatically. This is why the staunchest opponents of any term-limit initiative are incumbent politicians and those in their orbit—backers, special interests, and staffers. If left up to them, they would have things proceed as they always have. Full steam ahead, no matter how out of touch that thinking is with that of the average voter and taxpayer.

Though there are occasional exceptions, as a rule, congressional elections have become less and less competitive, and along with this we can see the decline of compromise and bipartisanship. When you think about it, the business of politics, as we have come to know it, is completely unlike that of any other industry or enterprise. This is because those on the inside control the rules of engagement—in other words the rules of competition. It is not something guided by the principles created by Mr. Madison and company, but rather a law unto itself. And the result is a system dominated by self-interest, not the public interest.

Think of it like this: Congress is a business, and we are the customers or clients. But not all customers are equal. Donors and other backers are special customers. Powerful ones. Now, in a private enterprise, ignoring most customers in favor of a few would ensure the demise of your business. That's what happens when real competition is taken out of the mix. But when competition is robust, customers have better options, and vice versa. In other words, everybody wins. But because competition is either absent or minimized when it comes to Congress and perpetual incumbency, most of us lose.

As citizens, we have the right to expect good solutions from Capitol Hill, but we often have to settle for political breadcrumbs. Whatever competition there is tends only to help politicians and their parties. Rivalry is confused with competition. Therefore, the system as we know it today must change. And the best way to start is congressional term limits. After all, look at what happened after 1994 and the Contract with America. Would what was started back then have fared better through the years had the term limits part of that contract succeeded? I think so.

Implementing term limits would be the best possible reform of our clearly broken system. What we have right now was designed by our elected representatives and largely for their own benefit. It has devolved over time (entropy), and I'm sure most Americans missed what was happening. But we have the power to change things. And we have a great tool for that change—congressional term limits.

Critics of term limits love to talk about how we already have them. They pause, presumably for effect, and then deliver the punch line: "They're called elections." Chortle, chortle. But how many of those elections are competitive? Ask the critics, and they'll pause indefinitely. When it comes to the Congress, our elections are inherently unfair. The deck is stacked against challengers—incumbency grants several percentage points of advantage from the start. A challenger starts way behind, and only a few can overcome that. It's simply a political fact.

Conservative author George Will wrote about "a perpetual incumbency machine," adding, "term limits are needed as an auxiliary precaution against the perennial lust for power." He regarded "careerism" as "the shared creed of Democrats and Republicans."[2] Term limits strike at the heart of the entrenched power of seniority. They also weaken the power of party leaders. Unlimited terms is the dominant culture in Congress. Removing that as a motive would be a giant leap toward authentic reform. After all, there is a clear and direct relationship between professional politicians and increased levels of government spending.

There is much talk in this country about how America needs to be more competitive globally. The best way to make that happen is for America to be more competitive in its elections. Maybe instituting term limits wouldn't be a panacea (though it would surely be close), but they have the potential to reform our political system and return power to the American people—where it is supposed to reside.

Oil Change

Your family automobile requires regular oil changes to keep the engine running smoothly and prevent sludge buildup. It's the same with the engine of Congress. Changing its "oil" (read: membership) on a regular basis not only protects the engine of government, but it also prevents the buildup of political sludge—a pretty good euphemism for the ugly side of politics.

Sludge in this metaphor can represent all kinds of

corruption, from the subtle version of Washington insider trading to the not-so-subtle kind that means money. And then, there's the sludge that represents the long-term buildup of outdated policies and perspectives.

Those who know all about car engines will tell you to change the oil regularly. How often will vary based on many factors, but one thing is clear—you can't have an oil change too often. It is cited as one of the best ways to ensure the health of your vehicle, likely one of your most significant investments. Toward that end, those who build our cars came up with a simple but effective way to remind us about this important vehicle maintenance imperative.

The old (and long-defunct) Hudson Motor Company came up with the first version way back in the 1930s.[3] It was dubbed the "idiot light." But years later, wiser marketing minds devised a better name—*the check engine light*. However, in fairness, if you ignore the one on your car's dashboard, the original name for it actually fits better. By the 1990s, it was a standard feature on new cars. Before that, you had to watch the dashboard gauges.

Term limits would create a political check engine light on the dashboard of American politics, an illuminated reminder of the need to change Congress's oil. Oh yeah. And just as a failure to regularly change your car's oil will (not might, but *will*) lead to disaster, a failure to change the makeup of Congress on a regular basis (via term limits) will have consequences. We might even blow a national gasket.

I suppose it's part of human nature to be uncomfortable with change—even resistant to it. We find the familiar comfortable. We tend to thrive on things like routine, tradition, and custom. All of this is relatively benign. But it's different when it comes to politics and government. As Jordan Peterson says, "If you stand still, you fall backwards. You cannot stand still because the world moves away from you if you stand still. And there is no stasis. Only backwards."[4]

Now, there's a good backward and a bad backward. The bad one involves being so stuck in the past (and present, even) that you refuse to even budge toward the next thing. By the way, this is a particular issue with our older citizens, some of whom have been in powerful government positions for quite a long time.

But there's also a good backward, and for the purposes of what I'm talking about in this book, it's the only way forward. That may sound paradoxical (or would that be oxymoronic?), but the best way for America to move forward politically is to move backward. The best political strategy for the twenty-first century is to take a fact-finding trip to the final decades of the eighteenth century. It is a "back-to-the-future" approach. And it's the best way to neutralize revisionist calls for us to see the Constitution as a so-called "living" document, which to them means the ability to make it say and mean whatever is politically advantageous today. That approach is inherently dismissive and disrespectful. It's also dangerous.

Advocates of the living constitution nonsense tell us that the Framers had no way of predicting how the United States would change over time, so what they crafted in 1787 must become like silly putty—flexible, moldable, and relevant. But they miss the obvious—the Framers included the amendment process in Article V. An amendment could be added by two-thirds of both Houses of Congress or by a convention called upon by two-thirds of the states. For it to be ratified and added to the Constitution, three-fourths of the states' legislatures would have to vote for the amendment. It would be a complex process, but the Constitution could be altered, just not by political whim. This method has worked well. The amendments that have been added down through the years prove that it is not impossible to adapt the Constitution to modern times. That's the real "living" Constitution at work. In other words, while the Constitution is not designed to address politics, it contains a framework to solve significant problems.

Limited Warranty

Let me give you one final lesson from my life in the automotive business. New vehicles come with a limited warranty to ensure they serve well for a given period of time. After that period expires, maintenance and repair become more challenging, less efficient, and more expensive. Similarly, a term limit could serve as a kind of warranty, ensuring that representatives remain effective and in touch with their constituents for a reasonable time frame.

The keyword is *limited*.

Congress functions these days under pretty much a full warranty, one that seems to cover everything. But with term limits in place, that would change, and so would much of the political arrogance and entitlement we see in American politics. When a car gets old and parts become hard to find, it's harder to get the thing fixed. Most people opt to trade in the old model for a newer one—one that has a limited warranty. But it seems like many in Congress want us to continue to "cover" them long after they should have been traded in.

Right?

I'm sure that you can find similar examples of real-world business practices that would benefit the American political process. That's because, as President Calvin Coolidge, a man known for his economy of words, once said, "The business of this country is business."

Instituting term limits for members of Congress would function as a political limited warranty. It would be an extension and compelling expression of the Framers' idea of limited government, a political system where restrictions are placed on the government to protect individual rights and liberties. This was a conscious departure from the British monarchy, which the men assembled in Philadelphia felt violated their rights. They deliberately designed a limited government that would have to abide by rules designed by the people.

And when it comes to the need for term limits as part of a larger limited political warranty for government, remember the words of economist Milton Friedman, "Keep your eye on one thing and one thing only: how much government is spending." To govern ourselves effectively, we must be vigilant, and we must hold our representatives accountable.

★ ★ ★

CHAPTER NINE

ARTICLE V

"The basis of our political system is the right of the people to make and alter their constitutions of government."
—George Washington

IN THE WAKE OF THE HOUSE'S FAILURE TO PASS TERM-LIMIT LEGISLATION IN THE SPRING OF 1995, the issue being the only part of the Contract with America not successfully translated into law, House Speaker Newt Gingrich vowed to present it to the next Congress. He planned to make the matter the centerpiece of another national congressional campaign in 1996.

But before he even got started, the Supreme Court gummed up the works.

The national grassroots trend toward limiting congressional tenure and returning the country to more of a citizen-legislator approach hit a major roadblock less than six weeks after term-limit legislation failed to pass muster on the House floor. That new barrier was a significant ruling by the U.S. Supreme Court in the case, U.S. Term Limits, Inc. v. Thornton, handed down on May 22, 1995. In a narrow five to four vote, the black-robed justices upheld the ruling of the highest court in Arkansas, striking a powerful blow against something the overwhelming majority of Americans supported—congressional term limits.

Never mind that 23 states had in recent years enacted various forms of term-limits legislation and that the national movement was approaching critical mass. They said Amendment 73 to the Arkansas constitution—adopted there in 1992—was not supported by the national constitution. Arkansas established term limits for those serving in both state and federal legislative offices. Writing for the majority, Justice John Paul Stevens argued:

> *The Constitution also provides that the qualifications of the representatives of each State will be judged by the representatives of the entire Nation. The Constitution thus creates a uniform national body representing the interests of a single people. Permitting individual States to formulate diverse qualifications for their representatives would result in a patchwork of state qualifications, undermining the uniformity and the national character that the Framers envisioned and sought to ensure.*[1]

But Clarence Thomas, representing the minority view, wrote:

> *Nothing in the Constitution deprives the people of each State of the power to prescribe eligibility requirements for the candidates who seek to represent them in Congress. The*

> *Constitution is simply silent on this question. And where the Constitution is silent, it raises no bar to action by the States or the people.*[2]

Liberals and others who wanted a big government led by political professionals heralded the ruling as a liberation day for the United States Congress. Most everyday Americans, however, saw it as the slap in the face it, in fact, was. The words in the preamble to the Arkansas rule the Supremes dismantled seemed ominously true: "Entrenched incumbency has led to an electoral system that is less free, less competitive, and less representative than the system established by the Founding Fathers."

Indeed.

Optimists said things like, "We came within one vote of winning the whole war." But that did little to brighten the national mood. Others vowed to fight on and took the long view. The Arkansas Attorney General expressed that idea, comparing the fight for term limits with the woman's suffrage movement. He said, "That took a number of years to come to fruition, and I believe the same will happen with term limits."

Yet here we are nearly 30 years later with no such fruit.

Interestingly, long forgotten now was something Justice Stephens said toward the end of his 61-page majority opinion. About the general idea of "rotation in office" he opined that it "may provide for the infusion of fresh ideas and new perspectives, and may decrease the likelihood that representatives will lose touch with their constituents," but I guess that really didn't matter in the end since it only made the case for what he and his colleagues had just undermined.

The Silver Lining

Though the whole issue of congressional term limits seemed for many (especially those opposed) to be dead on arrival, others saw a glimmer of hope in the landmark Supreme Court decision. Justice Stevens, in his wordy opinion, reminded Americans that such a change in politics du jour, "must not come by legislation adopted by Congress or by an individual state, but rather...through the amendment procedures." In other words, if something was deemed unconstitutional, the only remedy was to amend the constitution itself. The only way to get the job done for the American people is through a constitutional amendment properly passed under procedures set forth in Article V, which says:

> *The Congress, whenever two thirds of both Houses shall deem it necessary, shall propose Amendments to this Constitution, or, on the Application of the Legislatures of two thirds of the several States, shall call a Convention for proposing Amendments, which, in either Case, shall be valid to all Intents and Purposes, as Part of this Constitution, when ratified by the Legislatures of three fourths of the several States, or by Conventions in three fourths thereof, as the one or the other Mode of Ratification may be proposed by the Congress; Provided that no Amendment which may be made prior to the Year One thousand eight hundred and eight shall in any Manner affect the first and fourth Clauses in the Ninth Section of the first Article; and that no State, without its Consent, shall be deprived of its equal Suffrage in the Senate.*

And this is where we've been ever since.

I find it ironic, if not hypocritical, that those on the left talk so much about the so-called "living constitution," the idea that it's okay to use a more liberal method to interpret it as opposed to one driven by strict construction. So, instead of trying to figure out what it meant in the days of the Framers, which some today view as irrelevant—sort of a dead-letter approach—they interpret it in light of their own particular political bias.

But when it comes to some things, like term limits, they quickly retreat and hide behind the barrier of strict construction, as in the case of the 1995 ruling. Nice work if you can get it. Living constitution aficionados believe the Constitution is outdated and needs to get with the times. Never mind that it remains the oldest written constitution in use by any nation on the planet—just one testament to its significance and relevance.

Of course, changes have been made in the Constitution since it was signed in Philadelphia back in 1787 and sent to the states for ratification—the addition of the Bill of Rights, for example. And there was that time when a new amendment was added, only to be rescinded a few years later. That case—Prohibition—is often cited by liberals as an example of how the document is inherently flawed. But the adoption and later repeal of the Eighteenth Amendment is actually evidence of what can happen when "we the people" carefully deliberate about an issue over a protracted period. The Twenty-First Amendment (which repeals the Eighteenth Amendment) is proof that the system put in place by the Constitution works and benefits the public interest.

But liberals, in their endless quest for progress, seem to have little taste for *process*.

The U.S. Constitution is not the Bible. It is not divinely inspired or factually inerrant. It has been changed, and that option remains open to each generation of Americans. The Framers understood that, but they also understood that no part of it should be changed or enhanced apart from a process lending itself to careful thought, wise deliberation, and broad-range accountability.

The Framers anticipated that generations after them would, as Madison put it in *The Federalist*, make whatever "useful alterations will be suggested by experience." They set up an amendment process that called for great deliberation to ensure those enhancements represent the settled opinion of the American people. It's a tried-and-true process, one that has been used twenty-seven times with great success. And that is the surest pathway to congressional term limits. It is a tough hill to climb, but it can be done.

And I think it will be done.

This brings us back to Article V. There are two roads to the adoption of a constitutional amendment fixing term limits as the law of the land. It can be done by Congress itself or via a special convention called by the states for the purpose of proposing amendments. But no matter which method is used to propose an amendment, it must ultimately be ratified by three-fourths of the states, that magic number being 38. It's a process. A careful one. A slow one. And it's what makes the document a Constitution, not just a bunch of laws passed by a legislative body. The Framers, in effect, loaded the process with a couple of "super-majority" benchmarks designed to keep the process from becoming impulsive or frivolous.

To date, all amendments to the Constitution have taken

the congressional route. They were proposed by the Congress and sent to the states for ratification. The special state convention option has never been used—but there have been times when we came close. There have actually been hundreds of times an amending convention has been applied for—from all but a handful of the states. In recent years, the mechanism has been tried for a balanced-budget amendment.

And there was one time when it almost worked.

That was more than a hundred years ago, and it was a game-changer in American politics. For our nation's first 124 years, United States senators were not elected by the people directly, but instead appointed by their state legislatures. Though there had been stirrings on the issue throughout the nineteenth century, nothing really happened on that front until the twentieth century dawned and Progressive-movement thinking began to take hold. It was an issue driven by the states, and supporters chose to use the convention strategy laid out in Article V.

The interesting takeaway from all this was that as they neared the mark of having two-thirds of the states demand that special convention—having 30 of the required 31—Congress saw the handwriting on the wall and decided to act. They had been reluctant because Congress has always been reluctant to change anything that takes power away from politicians in favor of the people. Sound familiar? Some things never change. The Seventeenth Amendment, which instituted direct election of U.S. senators, was approved by Congress and sent to the states in 1912, and it was fully ratified a year later. In effect, the threat of a special convention option prodded Congress to do something it didn't want to do. Something against its very nature.

In the Senate, particularly, they refused to vote on the

matter because many of its members would have lost their jobs if they were required to win popular support, similar to how many of them refuse to support a term-limit amendment today for the same reason. The states, in effect, used the threat of a special convention to force Washington's hand.

It was powerful political leverage—and it can be again.

Because politicians are always averse to anything that threatens to rock their insulated boat and despise the idea of giving up the perks that accompany chronic incumbency, we can hardly expect them to act on term limits without being sufficiently "motivated." And Article V gives us a great motivational tool.

For those who think using the special convention clause in Article V is way "out there" and not something for serious people, I might remind them that one of the greatest Americans who ever lived thought it was a good idea. He had a great legal mind and was a pretty good politician too. You've surely heard of him—Abraham Lincoln.

That's right. Mr. Lincoln, at the very moment he was stepping onto the stage as president of the United States during a time of national crisis, knew things needed to change and the Constitution would have to be amended to make it happen. He had studied both pathways to the process described in Article V, and during his first inaugural address on March 4, 1861, had this to say on the subject:

> *I will venture to add that, to me, the convention mode seems preferable, in that it allows amendments to originate with the people themselves, instead of only permitting them to take, or reject, propositions, originated by others, not especially chosen*

> *for that purpose, and which might not be precisely such, as they would wish to either accept or refuse.*[3]

Honest Abe, who had a way with words, nailed it.

Now, any discussion with an opponent of the idea of creating an Article V convention for a term-limits amendment to the Constitution will quickly lead to an objection they think should end the matter. It goes something like this: "Well, that's just opening a Pandora's box. You'd have a runaway convention and if they wanted to scrap the whole Bill of Rights, they could. It's just too risky. In fact, it's downright dangerous." This evokes an image of some kind of free-for-all that could lead to a national meltdown. But it's *that* argument that's the dangerous one.

The idea of a so-called "runaway" convention is simply a myth. Worse, it is a straw man. It's designed to shut the conversation down. After all, who in their right mind would want to scrap the whole U.S. Constitution? Of course, no one other than an America-hating anarchist would. But it does beg a response, if only to keep the focus where it belongs—the best path to serious term-limit reform.

Opponents of using the special convention option put in place by the Framers are fond of insisting that such a convention could not be limited to one issue. If the delegates decided they wanted to, they could set out to revise the entire Constitution. They like to remind us that we wouldn't want to put the Bill of Rights at risk, though presumably some on the left might want to gut that pesky Second Amendment.

But the "putting the whole Constitution at risk" argument is specious and cannot stand up. There are clear restraints built into Article V that make this clear. Let me state unequivocally here that it would be impossible to rewrite any part of the U.S. Constitution against the wishes of the American people. Period.

No Article V convention needs to have a broad scope or become a populist fishing expedition. There is no way it could be repealed. A careful reading of the actual words framed in 1787 does not in any way refer to rewriting or revising the Constitution. It specifically talks about proposing *amendments*, and amendments have been proposed since even before the ratification of the original document. The Bill of Rights came to be not long after the Constitution was put in force. They were in the form of amendments. Amendments are good things and have helped our nation grow. The process involved in adding amendments to the Constitution is solid and secure. They are modifications, not revisions.

Madison and the others gathered in Philadelphia that summer long ago weren't afraid of Article V—even the convention provision. In *The Federalist* no. 85, Alexander Hamilton wrote: "There can be no comparison between the facility of effecting an amendment and that of establishing, in the first instance, a complete Constitution." Clearly, the Framers understood that Article V amendments weren't constitutional "rewrites," and we should too. In fact, when you think about it, the whole "living Constitution" idea so prevalent today is much more in line with rewriting the whole thing.

The security is, as is usually the case, in the safeguards put in place by the Framers. The intent is clear. Such a convention would be for the purpose of proposing amendments. It would have no purpose or authority beyond that. First, the process is restrained by the ratification requirement. Any amendment proposed by a special convention created under Article V must be ratified by 38 of the 50 states—a high hurdle indeed. So even in the hypothetical (and ludicrously unlikely) scenario of a constitutional convention run amok, its fruit would have to be approved by three-fourths of the states in the union. Does anyone honestly think a really bad idea can scale that mountain?

History is clear on this. Ratifying an amendment is seldom a slam dunk. Look at the Equal Rights Amendment. It languished below the ratification threshold for decades. Can anyone seriously suggest that a plank of nonsensical and anti-Constitution amendments designed to subvert things could pass muster? Give me a break. The only way a dramatic rewriting of the Constitution could happen would be if an overwhelming majority of Americans wanted it.

Like I said, it's a straw man argument.

As my friend, Senator Tommy Tuberville, puts it: "I long supported a constitutional amendment requiring congressional term limits as an outsider, and now that I've been on the inside for a while, I am even more convinced we need it."

Related to the ratification requirement is the ratification *process*. Remember, if somehow, someway, during a zombie apocalypse, crazy people managed to propose amendments, there would still be another layer of protection—Congress itself. Article V is clear—Congress controls just how the amendments are ratified. Congress can choose whether it can be done through state legislatures or through state conventions.

If the latter option is chosen, citizens would elect delegates to represent them, providing even more power to the people. The benefit of this would be that those elected as delegates would be on the record as to the issue of ratification of a specific amendment. Those already seated in legislatures would not necessarily be on the record. The thinking is that citizens would not know where the legislators stand on the issue in question. The bottom line is that the fact that Congress chooses the method of ratification is another safeguard against a so-called "runaway convention." Congress would also be able to enact procedures to guide such a convention.

Earlier, I mentioned that the option for proposing amendments via a convention called for by the states has never been used. But what is sometimes missed by opponents of the idea is that it has been used during the ratification process. The first twenty times the Constitution was amended, ratification took place via state legislatures. But when it came to the amendment designed to repeal an earlier one—number eighteen about Prohibition—Congress chose to have special state conventions called to ratify it.

Herbert Hoover described Prohibition as "a great social and economic experiment, noble in motive and far-reaching in purpose." Some historians still refer to it as "The Noble Experiment." By the time it became the law of the land via the Eighteenth Amendment to the Constitution, the anti-alcohol movement had been around for decades. In fact, it was a big part of the Progressive agenda back then (read: liberal agenda). Supporters saw a strong link between corruption in society and beverage alcohol. It was a moral cause, but even more, one that was seen as beneficial to the American economy. Until it wasn't.

The story of the 1920s is ironic and filled with the kind of excess, crime, and corruption that Prohibition was designed to remedy. And by the time the stock market tanked, the mood in

America had changed, and the clock started ticking on Prohibition. By 1932, the platforms of both Republican and Democrat parties contained planks calling for its repeal. Congress followed suit and passed the Twenty-First Amendment to send to the forty-eight states. However, instead of sending it to the various state legislatures, it was decided to bypass the state houses and use the state convention option for the first time in our nation's history. The thinking was that this method allowed people to choose delegates for this single issue and not have it distorted by the larger agenda at play in state capitals. In effect, these conventions would be ad hoc committees designed to deal with one thing.

The ratification process provides an important and often overlooked (or ignored) case study in how the state convention option allowed for in Article V can and did work. Critics today say that Article V is too vague and leaves many unanswered questions. But one thing is certain—the state conventions back then functioned wonderfully and clearly demonstrated what can be accomplished when the objective is clear.

I would prefer to see Congress itself propose a term-limits amendment, but unless enough like-minded members are elected in a system rigged toward perpetuating incumbency, I don't see that happening. So, it is clear to me that the best option available is a movement among the states of our union that would then petition the U.S. Congress to convene a convention. Sure, it's a serious step and not one to be taken lightly, but it may be the only way for the American people to get the change they very much want. And no amount of misinformation or propaganda should get in the way.

The late Supreme Court Justice Antonin Scalia put it this way:

> *The Founders inserted this alternative method of obtaining constitutional amendments because they knew the Congress would be unwilling to give attention to many issues the people are concerned with, particularly those involving restrictions on the federal government's own power. The founders foresaw that and provided the convention as a remedy...Three-quarters of the states would have to ratify whatever came out of the convention; therefore, I don't worry much about it. I would also be willing to run that risk for issues primarily involving the structure of the federal government and a few other so-called single issues.*[4]

Of course, the great jurist was right.

CHAPTER TEN

BUT WHAT ABOUT...?

"Too many in Washington display a ruling class mentality, and congressional term limits would go a long way towards restoring the citizen-legislator ethos of the Founding Fathers."
—Ron DeSantis

EVEN THOUGH EVERY SURVEY INDICATES BROAD-BASED AND OVERWHELMING SUPPORT for implementing congressional term limits, the idea has its critics. Most naysayers are either elected officials, those who work for those officials, or political scientists who pontificate from the ivory towers of predominantly liberal academia. They ignore the will of the people because they think they know better. Actually, they think they know *best*.

But their objections are worth noting and deserve a response. There are just a few, but the opponents of term-limits reform keep them alive and kicking. These objections have been noted elsewhere in this book, but I want to summarize them as well as my responses.

We Already Have Term Limits— They're Called Elections

This is the most common anti-term-limits retort. And it is the one that resonates best with many Americans. It sounds like basic common sense. After all, we go to the polls every two years to vote for someone to represent us in the House of Representatives. We can decide to limit the terms of anyone by simply not voting them into office or voting them out. But it's easier said than done as the system now functions.

As propaganda, the argument is compelling. As a matter of policy, it doesn't work. It is, at best, a political smokescreen deliberately designed to cloud reality. Professional politicians of all stripes and from both major parties use it as one of their preferred tactics in their ongoing effort to protect their fiefdom.

Elections, though an important element of our constitutional republic, are not played out on level playing fields in American congressional districts. The deck is stacked in favor of incumbents throughout the country. And unless there is some anomalous factor—a scandal, political upheaval, or some such thing—the person holding the office will almost always win over the person seeking to replace that person. In 2022, congressional incumbents had a 98% win rate.[1] And in 41 states, 100% of the incumbents running for reelection to the House of Representatives were victorious. A good number of the races weren't even close to competitive. Was this kind of success a referendum on how Americans feel about Congress? No way. Poll after poll indicates increasing frustration and distrust with Washington politicians.

A March 2023 survey conducted by the University of Maryland School of Public Policy indicated 83% of Americans favored passing a constitutional amendment to establish term limits in Congress. And it seems to be a bipartisan sentiment, with 86% of Republicans, 80% of Democrats, and 84% of Independents in agreement.

Incumbents have access to PAC money, 90% of which flows toward them. After all, they spend a lot of their time raising those funds in the first place. Newcomers usually begin funding their campaigns with their own money. There are no limits, but it must be reported.

It's common for a new candidate to put up tens of thousands of dollars of their own money to get a campaign off the ground. If they can pick up traction, it's possible to pick up increasing support along the way, while the incumbent they seek to unseat typically has the capacity to outspend a challenger tenfold.

If somehow, someway, a challenger manages to pull off a miracle and beat the incumbent, when the time for reelection comes around, most put up none of their own money. Do the math. The system is not fair at all. Elections are not term limits. They are far from competitive and only by putting term limits in place can they become so.

Term Limits Are Anti-Democratic

On the contrary, term limits would free democracy from the stranglehold of lobbyists and special interests. Just follow the money, and you'll see this. Congressional careerists love to talk the talk when it comes to democracy, but walking the walk is another matter entirely. The way the system runs now is anti-democratic.

The argument that term limits undermine democratic principles is another favorite of professional politicians. It treats the voters with contempt disguised as condescension.

Term limits would be a move toward the Constitution and away from congressional careerism. They would enhance democracy. Are we less of a democracy because no president can serve more than two terms? Or does our democracy function better because we have more options?

Some might argue that when we can't vote for someone because they cannot run for another term, our democracy suffers. Really? It's okay to hold a leader or public servant in high esteem, but shouldn't we be careful not to put them on permanent pedestals? If professional politicians are so concerned about democracy, why the reluctance to vote on something that more than 80% of Americans clearly want?

Term limits are in no way undemocratic. They are, in fact, the best way for us to preserve, protect, and defend democratic principles and practices in our beloved constitutional republic.

With Term Limits, We'd Lose Experienced Legislators

This argument springs from the "indispensable man" line of thought. The idea is that we need people with experience running things in Washington. I agree. However, the experienced people we need are from the real world rather than the world inside the Beltway. I love Ronald Reagan's perspective on this.

He often remarked that the only experience you get in politics is how to be political.

Washington experience is not the kind of experience we need. A better way would be to support a process that would bring the best minds to bear on public policy and the public's purse strings. Term limits would lead to more and more people with experience in the real world having a chance to bring that experience to the congressional table.

Who would be better dealing with a matter relating to American businesses, an actual person from the business world or a professional politician? How about healthcare policy—a physician or professional politician? I think you get my point.

I think what we see these days in Congress makes the best case that the so-called "experienced" people who are determined to hold onto power as long as they can don't have the kind of experience the nation needs. Sure, there was a time in our country's early days when there were fewer educated people. Maybe back then, a case could be made that rotation in office might hurt the idea of having intelligent people in charge, but I'm pretty sure the country has grown enough in a couple of hundred years to ensure a significant pool of talent and expertise to meet our needs. We can, at any time, find 535 of the best and brightest when we need them. Term limits will give us a better chance to discover new talent.

The idea that political professionals function as some kind of elite American aristocracy and they know what is "best" for the rest of us is nothing more than political hubris. I mean, just do the math—each congressional district in America represents around 760,000 people. Do the members of Congress actually think they are the only ones capable of serving their constituencies? Come to think of it, they probably do, and that's more than sad—it's pathetic.

Speaking of the math, those "experienced" politicians who know better than the rest of us have led us down the path toward financial ruin by putting us more than $33 trillion (that's trillion with a "t", as in timebomb) in debt. Or better stated, they've put that burden on our children and grandchildren, and more generations to follow. I, for one, say it's time to reform the system that gives us all these "experienced" politicians because the only experience they seem to have is a collective ability to make irresponsible choices and somehow manage to stay in their jobs.

Term Limits Are Unconstitutional

The answer to this objection is, well, yes, the Supreme Court ruled in 1995 on this. But that didn't end the matter at all. First, that ruling was issued by a five to four vote. Hardly decisive. And what they did in no way precludes the Constitution itself from being amended. The adoption and ratification of a constitutional term-limits amendment would make them constitutional—ipso facto. And five out of every six Americans favor such an amendment. That's Republicans, Democrats, and Independents. By the way, if the case from 1995 was ruled on by the Supreme Court today, does anyone doubt the outcome would be different?

Supreme Court Justice Neil Gorsuch wrote about the issue long before his appointment to the nation's highest court. It's pretty clear how he'd see the issue today. He argued:

> *The text of the Constitution leaves room for term limits. Article I, section 4, explicitly grants the states wide latitude to determine the times, places, and manner of congressional elections. This provision, in our judgment, fully empowers states to enforce term limits on members of their congressional delegations. Moreover, a term limit is harmonious with our constitutional guarantees of free speech or equal protection.*[2]

If some see term limits for members of Congress as unconstitutional, then let's go ahead and actually put them in the Constitution.

CHAPTER ELEVEN

TERM LIMITS FOR THE SUPREME COURT?

"The framers of the Constitution were so clear in The Federalist Papers *and elsewhere that they felt an independent judiciary was critical to the success of the nation."*
—Sandra Day O'Conner

THIS OBJECTION—THE NOTION OF APPLYING TERM LIMITS TO THE SUPREME COURT—DESERVES ITS OWN CHAPTER. It's a topic that recently gained attention and traction. It comes up often, especially when some public figure disagrees with a court decision. But any examination of this requires a basic understanding of how the three branches of our government—the executive, the judicial, and the legislative— work, or at least are supposed to work. Congress is, of course, the legislative branch. It includes the House of Representatives and the Senate. It is designed to represent the voices of the American people. Term limits would ensure the regular influx of new perspectives and prevent the establishment of political fiefdoms. This would help to keep it dynamic and responsive.

The Framers designed a system with three distinct branches that provided checks among themselves. Any attempt toward political limits on the judicial branch could have unintended consequences. Beyond this, special interests have a powerful reach into the legislative branch because of the "power of the purse." This is not the case with SCOTUS. The judicial branch has an inherent responsibility to maintain its independence as a critical check against overreach on the part of the other two branches.

While limiting the number of terms a member of Congress can serve may spur them to action, I believe we want our courts to be more measured and less reactive to the vicissitudes of partisan politics. The Supreme Court must be entirely focused on the foundation of law and the Constitution. Knowing that their time in office would be limited might push judiciary members to make more reckless, even radical rulings.

The most fundamental reason, however, to be hesitant about term limits for Supreme Court justices centers around the importance of judicial independence, consistency in interpretation, understanding the differing roles of the branches of government, and the increased likelihood of further polarization and politicization of the nominating process.

Federalist No. 78 says,

> *If, then, the courts of justice are to be considered as the bulwarks of a limited Constitution against legislative encroachments, this consideration will afford a strong argument for the permanent tenure of judicial offices since nothing will contribute so much as this to that independent spirit in the judges which must be essential to the faithful performance of so arduous a duty.*

And Federalist No. 79 adds:

> *The precautions for their responsibility are comprised in the article respecting impeachments. They are liable to be impeached for misconduct by the House of Representatives, and tried by the Senate; and, if convicted, may be dismissed from office, and disqualified for holding any other. This is the only provision on the point which is consistent with the necessary independence of the judicial character, and is the only one which we find in our own Constitution in respect to our own judges. The want of a provision for removing the judges on account of inability has been a subject of complaint. But all considerate men will be sensible that such a provision would either not be practiced upon or would be more liable to abuse than calculated to answer any good purpose. The mensuration of the faculties of the mind has, I believe, no place in the catalogue of known arts. An attempt to fix the boundary between*

the regions of ability and inability, would much oftener give scope to personal and party attachments and enmities than advance the interests of justice or the public good. The result, except in the case of insanity, must for the most part be arbitrary; and insanity, without any formal or express provision, may be safely pronounced to be a virtual disqualification.

So I want to make the following points:

- **Judicial Independence**—The lifetime tenure of Supreme Court justices is designed to shield the court from the vagaries of public opinion and political pressure. This independence ensures they can make decisions based on law and precedent, not political expediency.

- **Consistency in Interpretation**—Having a stable court ensures consistency in legal interpretation. Regular turnover might lead to more frequent and dramatic shifts in legal doctrine, potentially causing unpredictability in the legal system.

- **Differing Roles**—While Congress is meant to be directly responsive to the people's will, the Court's role is to be an impartial interpreter of the laws. This fundamental difference underscores why term limits may be more appropriate for one body and not the other.

- **Nomination Battles**—Given the high stakes of each Supreme Court seat, predictable, regular vacancies due to term limits could make the nomination and confirmation processes even more contentious and politicized than they currently are.

There are other ways to keep the Supreme Court accountable while maintaining its independence. The Constitution provides checks and balances even for lifetime appointments. Impeachment, though a drastic measure, is one such mechanism. While it should be used carefully and with due caution, it's an essential tool to ensure members of the highest court in the land perform their duties effectively.

While it has not been used on a Supreme Court justice since 1804, it has been used many times on other federal judges. In 1804, Justice Samuel Chase was impeached by the House of Representatives. The charges against him stemmed more from political disagreements and his judicial conduct rather than any specific criminal acts. His impeachment seemed to have been motivated primarily by Thomas Jefferson's Democratic-Republicans, who were frustrated with the Federalist slant of the courts and looked to assert more control.

However, when the trial reached the Senate in 1805, Chase was acquitted of all charges. The Senate did not secure the necessary two-thirds majority to remove him from office. The case of Samuel Chase established an important precedent: Justices should not be impeached for political reasons or based on disagreements with their judicial decisions. This ensures the independence of the judiciary. Since then, no Supreme Court justice has been impeached, but several federal judges have been impeached and removed from the bench.[1]

We should work to encourage a culture where justices, recognizing their own limitations, choose to step down when they feel they can't serve with the same vigor as before. This would require careful messaging and respect for a justice's decades of service.

Any mechanisms of accountability, whether impeachment or medical evaluations, are not about challenging the court's independence. Instead, they're about ensuring the court continues to serve its purpose as outlined in the Constitution—as a body of clear-thinking, unbiased interpreters of the law. While at some point, we may need to further examine the structure of the court and explore term limits or implement a mandatory retirement age, addressing the issue of Congress is much more critical.

Here's a list of some of the federal judges removed via impeachment:

- **John Pickering, District Court Judge**—Impeached in 1803 for chronic intoxication and unlawful rulings. He was convicted by the Senate and removed from office in 1804.

- **West Humphreys, District Court Judge**—Impeached in 1862 for refusing to hold court and for waging war against the U.S. government. He was convicted by the Senate and removed later that year.

- **Robert W. Archbald, Commerce Court Judge**—Impeached in 1912 for improper business relationships with litigants. He was convicted by the Senate and removed in 1913.

- **Halsted Ritter, District Court Judge**—Impeached in 1936 for multiple reasons, including showing favoritism in appointments and practicing law while a judge. He was convicted and removed from office later that year.

- **Harry E. Claiborne, District Court Judge**—Impeached in 1986 for tax evasion. He was convicted by the Senate and removed from office the same year. Notably, he was the first federal judge to be sent to prison.

- **Walter L. Nixon, District Court Judge**—Impeached in 1989 for perjury before a grand jury. Even though he had been previously convicted in a criminal court and was serving time in prison, Nixon refused to resign from his position. The Senate subsequently convicted and removed him from office.

- **Alcee Hastings, District Court Judge**—Impeached in 1988 for perjury and conspiring to solicit a bribe. He was acquitted in a criminal court but was later convicted by the Senate and removed from office in 1989. Interestingly, after his removal, Hastings was elected to the U.S. House of Representatives and served there for several terms.

- **Thomas Porteous, District Court Judge**—Impeached in 2010 for bribery and perjury. He was convicted and removed from office by the Senate the same year.

These cases emphasize the gravity of the impeachment process and highlight the standards to which federal judges are held. When federal judges engage in misconduct, impeachment remains a potent tool for ensuring the integrity of the judiciary.

Throwing the notion of term limits for Supreme Court justices into the vital discussion about congressional term limits is, at best, a distraction. At worst, it is a cynical effort to undermine the clear will of the American people. Nancy Pelosi's pronouncements on the subject are an example of contemptuous politics run amok and beyond mere irony. The former Speaker of the House of Representatives is a poster child for congressional careerism but has no problem with the idea of limiting how long someone can serve on the Supreme Court. "There certainly should be terms limits" for the nation's highest court, she insists, because it would help to hold it accountable.[2] Never mind the fact that she is running for yet another term that would extend her time in her seat to nearly 40 years. Pelosi turned 83 in March 2023.

Cleary Pelosi is busy "making the world safe for hypocrisy," to quote the late novelist Thomas Wolfe.

The bottom line is this—the American people want term limits for members of Congress. Members of Congress don't. It's time for the American people to rise up and show the professional politicians just who is actually in charge of the United States of America—we the people.

The arguments for congressional term limits—even presidential ones—do not apply well to the case of our nation's highest court. The executive and legislative branches of government are designed to be driven by political processes called elections. And even though without term limits, congressional elections are far from fair, they are still essential to our republic. To put term limits on how long a Supreme Court justice can serve would politicize the role in a way the Framers never intended.

We've noted how the men who launched this country were students of history. They were thus keenly aware that there was a time when English judges served at the pleasure of the monarch. But during the seventeenth century, the people rose up and the result was legislation making judicial tenure a life term. This was done to ensure judicial independence. The idea was that judges functioned best away from the rough and tumble of politics. Their focus must be on the law.

Let's be frank. The current uptick in calls for Supreme Court term limits is a direct result of the 2022 ruling overturning Roe v. Wade. And that whole matter was politicized in ways never before seen in this country, from the leak of a pre-ruling document to the illegal stalking of the homes of the justices. Is that the best climate for serious judicial deliberation? Do we want the court politicized? I mean, just look at the circus atmosphere when a new justice is nominated and up for approval by Congress.

Political factors are in the very DNA of the executive and legislative branches—they should be nowhere near the judicial branch, otherwise it would cease to be independent and would become dependent on the whims of the other two. Advocates of Supreme Court term limits also argue that rotating justices more often would ensure the court kept up with political realities in the nation. The thinking is that long-serving justices tend to be tied to the politics of yesteryear. But that dog won't hunt because it fails to factor in the main function of our judicial system, which has very much to do with the prevention of vacillating political majorities from treading on the rights of others. In effect, the judicial branch of government is in place to guard against the tyranny of the majority.

Here's the bottom line—congressional term limits would make the legislative branch function as the Framers intended. Supreme Court term limits, on the contrary, would lead to the judicial branch functioning in ways the Framers never intended or envisioned. It's a bad idea. The whole issue is a distraction and diversion. There is no real comparison whatsoever.

Like apples and oranges.

CHAPTER TWELVE

TOWARD A CONGRESS OF CITIZEN LEGISLATORS

"*Most of the founders of this country had day jobs for years. They were not career politicians. We need leaders with experience in the real world, not experience in the phony world of politics.*"
—Thomas Sowell

THOUGH THIS BOOK IS ABOUT THE NEED FOR CONGRESSIONAL TERM LIMITS, implementing this vital reform will be a giant leap for the American people. It is not the end game but a powerful means toward the end. The end is a legislative branch that functions the way the Framers meant. The end game is limited government. The end game is giving power back to the people. And all of this means the end game is a citizen legislature.

Now, when many hear about the idea of a citizen legislature, their heads start to spin, and their imaginations conjure images of rural America and small towns and farmers leaving their plows to serve part-time for little or no pay and then when their work is done head back to those plows. Of course, that happened in America a couple of centuries ago. Could that practice apply to our nation today? The answer is yes, but only with some modifications and common-sense considerations. The knee-jerk way to approach the citizen-legislator idea is to simply dismiss it as an archaic notion irrelevant to modern cultural and political realities. As usual, knee-jerk responses may be reflexive, but they aren't all that helpful.

When discussing citizen legislators and how term limits would move Congress toward becoming more of a citizen legislature, I am not advocating a part-time, low-pay, or no-pay body. We certainly need our Congress to work full-time (such as it is) on the needs and problems of everyday Americans. America is not a small town—it's a colossus. America could not function with a legislative body working a few months out of the year like a few smaller states. In fact, America needs a legislature that spends all of its time on the people's business—the thing politicians always say they want—rather than their own business (read: preparing for the next election).

A Congress filled with citizen legislators would get more of the people's business done—and much better.

Of Framers and Farmers

While the Framers chose not to incorporate the idea of "rotation in office" in 1787, it's clear from their writings that they understood the importance of people limiting time in office. They just assumed reasonable and responsible public servants would police themselves. They were wrong, of course, maybe even naive, considering their views of human nature, but their error is one we can fix.

Thomas Jefferson penned these words in a letter to a member of the Virginia House of Delegates in 1797: "All [reforms] can be done peaceably, by the people confining their choice of Representatives and Senators to persons attached to republican government and the principles of 1776; not office-hunters, but farmers whose interests are entirely agricultural. Such men are the true representatives of the great American interest and are alone to be relied on for expressing the proper American sentiments." [Emphasis added][1] And a few months before he was elected as our third president, he wrote this in a letter to his old revolutionary comrade Samuel Adams: "A government by representatives elected by the people at short periods was our object, and our maxim... was, 'where annual election ends, tyranny begins.'"[2]

The reference to farmers is what confuses critics of a citizen legislature. Two hundred years ago, more than half of the American population was made up of farmers. It was the primary engine driving the nation's economy. The country was primarily rural. Of course, it's far from that today. So, because most Americans aren't farmers, does that make Jefferson's ideas obsolete? Of course not. Farmers in 1800 were hard-working everyday citizens. The last time I looked, the American economy continued to be driven by hard-working ordinary citizens. Jefferson's point was not agricultural; it was cultural. If it helps, read that quote again, but switch out the word "farmers" for any other career today.

Real-World Experience

A Congress made up of citizen legislators would bring firsthand experience in the real world to bear on problems and policies. There's a clear advantage to having professionals and business leaders from the private sector serving as legislators. Too often, policies are based on what lawyers and politicians think best. We need representatives who truly understand the industries and businesses they regulate.

I ran a Honda store in Birmingham, Alabama, during the Cash for Clunkers program in 2009. Congress, in its infinite wisdom, had passed legislation designed to get older gas-guzzling cars off the roads and induce Americans to buy newer fuel-efficient models with a program of vouchers. Of course, we were excited to have a way to boost our sales during a challenging economic period—the Great Recession. But as with most government-initiated programs, the Cash for Clunkers program had more than its share of flaws. And many, if not most, of them could have been avoided if there had been some people with experience in the automotive industry helping to design the program.

The system was cumbersome. And so many quality vehicles that could have helped those at the bottom rungs of the economic ladder were destroyed. They were no longer on the market, and those with low incomes had fewer transportation options. It became a logistic nightmare. Vehicles that could have been affordable and reliable were no longer available because some woke elitists believed they knew best what Americans should be driving. Big trucks were terrible, to their thinking, as were other vehicles deemed "fuel inefficient," so arbitrary decisions were made about what could be traded and what Honda dealers had to buy.

Then, there were the late nights, as we spent seemingly endless hours trying to work with the government computer system. As a small business, we were dependent on cash flow, but at one point, we had more than $2 million in outstanding receivables from Washington. I have no doubt that having several members of Congress who had backgrounds in the automotive world could have helped that program. Or they could have developed a model that made more sense than sending tens of thousands of good cars to the crusher.

Congress needs leaders who understand what rules and regulations do to businesses. We need real-world leaders to help solve real-world problems instead of just creating more of them. Let me share several things citizen legislators would bring to Congress.

Practical Know-How

Congress is filled with self-proclaimed "experts" but is woefully lacking in hands-on experience. For example, since Congress manages the nation's purse, having people who knew about accounting could help. But there are only four accountants in the House in the 118th Congress. And how about representatives with a law-enforcement background? You'd think that, since Congress is about passing laws, knowing a thing or two about enforcing them would be helpful. Yet only four police officers are in the House right now.[3]

But there are plenty of people from the worlds of politics and law.

I love the story of George McGovern. Yes, that guy. The one who ran against Nixon in 1972 and served twenty-two years in the House and Senate. After he left politics, he invested most of his money in an inn in Connecticut. It had long been his dream to own such a place. But his dream turned into a nightmare. Years later, he wrote about it in the *Wall Street Journal*. He said:

> *In retrospect, I wish I had known more about the hazards and difficulties of such a business, especially during a recession of the kind that hit New England just as I was acquiring the inn's 43-year leasehold. I also wish that during the years I was in public office, I had had this firsthand experience about the difficulties business people face every day...my business associates and I also lived with federal, state and local rules that were all passed with the objective of helping employees, protecting the environment, raising tax dollars for schools, protecting our customers from fire hazards, etc. While I never have doubted the worthiness of any of these goals, the concept that most often eludes legislators is: 'Can we make consumers pay the higher prices for the increased operating costs that accompany public regulation and government reporting requirements with reams of red tape?' It is a simple concern that is nonetheless often ignored by legislators.*[4]

Capitol Hill is too far removed from the real world.

Economic Insight

How many professional politicians have ever had to manage a budget or meet a payroll? Not many—and surely not enough. Our representatives in Congress are supposed to have answers to questions about spending and the economy. Still, I wonder how many could pass an Econ 101 exam at the local community college. I don't usually find much of what Alexandria Ocasio-Cortez says to be very helpful. Still, this somewhat tortured sentence might come close: "I don't think most of Congress understands how economics works."[5]

The problem is that too many politicians are focused on macroeconomics, whereas most real-world Americans are focused on microeconomics. The distinction is important. Macroeconomics is about a large scale—national or global. That's important, sure, but real people live and work with the dynamics of microeconomics, which deals with individuals, businesses, and other issues that are close to home for people. The laws passed by Congress have a microeconomic impact for the most part. They hit us where we live.

Government policies indeed tend to be complex, but those in charge need to think first and foremost about how they impact individual lives. A Congress dominated by citizen legislators would be more inclined to remember this than one controlled by professional politicians. President Harry Truman used to say economists were hard to work with because they had too many hands; "they always say, on the one hand, and on the other hand."

Innovative Solutions

Business leaders are problem solvers. They have to be, otherwise, they wouldn't be in business, and they certainly wouldn't be leaders. If you've seen the movie Apollo 13, you know how NASA workers had to pull together to get an imperiled crew safely home after they'd had James Lovell described benignly as "a problem." In one great scene, the flight director Gene Krantz (played by Ed Harris) gathers a group of science and engineering geeks in a room and dumps a load of random items in front of them. They were the things the astronauts in space had to work with to rig a life-saving device that would remove carbon dioxide quickly. And repeatedly in the film, Kranz was heard to say: "Let's work the problem, people!"[6]

Those who run small businesses "work the problem" every day.

But when the primary "problem" those who represent us in Congress are preoccupied with is how to raise enough money to keep getting reelected, the institution itself has become a problem needing a solution. And that solution is for more and more citizen legislators to step forward to serve. But that's only possible if we can implement term limits.

Risk Management

Being willing to manage risk is essential in the real world. Decisions can have immediate consequences. But professional politicians are risk averse when it comes to making the tough decisions that often must be made. Risk management involves finding, assessing, and controlling threats to your business. The idea is that a company will consider all the areas that could result in a problem for them and the best ways to handle them.

A company that has heavy risk or doesn't have the management aspect worked out may find investors are not excited about giving money. They may also find that they run into more problems than they have money or time to fix. Taking risk management seriously can help a company be prepared for the future.

Could we use more of this in Congress? Oh yeah.

Yet, year after year, those representing us in Washington continue to put our collective future at risk with reckless spending and excessive regulation. They are all about the reward—politically—but seldom focus on the risks to everyday people.

Results Oriented

In the real world of business, results are crucial. Not so much in Washington, where kicking the political can down the road is the norm. Just look at how Congress deals with a pending budget crisis and deadline. Or the debt ceiling. Accountability—or better, a lack thereof—is directly related to how seriously results are pursued. When image and perception are the currency of the realm, it doesn't matter if you have actually done anything, only that it looks like you have.

When it comes to business, however, results are more than how the score is kept or about perception; they are the bottom line. As the saying goes, "What gets measured gets done." In politics, measuring anything is a challenge. Sending people to Congress with a proven track record of getting things done at home would be a great way to get things done there. But when a politician's primary "success" is as a politician, does that, at the end of the day (or the term), really mean anything?

President Truman came back from a double-digit deficit in the polls when he ran for re-election in 1948. He pulled off a political surprise by telling people at whistle-stops around the country that he was running against a "do-nothing Congress." The man from Missouri may be on to something that might work today. Congress is controlled by a system—committees, seniority, etc.—that produces few results. But that can change with term limits and an influx of citizen legislators.

Political Independence

When people with a track record of success and results in business are better able to run for and be elected to Congress (because of term limits), the House and Senate will include more people with the financial independence that immunizes them from the influences of special interests. They wouldn't have to curry favor and chase donations. Lobbyists would find them hard to "persuade."

And because they know term limits mean they will go back home after their specific tenure, the only people they feel obligated to are those who elected them in the first place. Anything that makes our representatives more immune to special interests is in the public interest.

We need outsiders in Washington who will never become "insiders." Political professionals are the perpetual insiders in Washington. They stay on the inside by convincing enough people that they have access to all the insider stuff the rest of us mere mortals can never have. They leverage that access into electoral success in election after election. But like the old Wizard of Oz, it's all just smoke and mirrors—the illusion that becomes delusion.

A fresh injection of outsider air is what Capitol Hill needs—citizen legislators.

Time to Step Up

As you can tell from what I've shared in this book, I've spent a great deal of time thinking about the state of politics in our country and how far we have drifted from our core constitutional values. And I have come to a decision.

I am going to serve.

I will take a few years—just a few—of my life to give something back to the country that has given me so much. I am willing to go from the private sector to public service. Emphasis on service. I want to be a true and faithful servant of and for the people, our Constitution, and our great future.

I am taking this step not because I am looking for a new career or to make a name for myself but to offer my talents and expertise—things proven in the business world—to my fellow citizens in the pursuit of the American dream of our forefathers.

I am fully aware that—as I have often noted in these chapters—the longer someone holds a public office, the greater the tendency to forget promises to serve a limited amount of time. But I also know that the longer someone breathes the rarified air inside the Beltway, the easier it is for corruption to eat away at a person's soul. I will not stay around Capitol Hill long enough for that to happen. That's a promise I am making to myself, my family, my future constituents, and ultimately to God.

I pledge to you that I will practice what I preach.

NOTES

[All quotes from *The Federalist Papers* are taken from the Dover Publications' June 2014 edition of *The Federalist Papers*. All quotes from Cato's Letters are taken from *Cato's Letters: Or Essays on Liberty, Civil and Religious, and Other Important Subjects,* Liberty Fund, Inc., July 1995.]

INTRODUCTION

1. https://founders.archives.gov/documents/Adams/99-02-02-3102.
2. *The Moral Basis of a Free Society*, by Steve Forbes, Hoover Institution, November 1, 1997.
3. *In the Arena: Reflections on Culture, History, Politics, and Faith*, David R. Stokes, p. 37.

CHAPTER ONE

1. *Cambridge Historical Journal*, Volume 6, Issue 3, 1940, pp. 307–321.
2. Genesis 6:4.
3. *The Man Who Would Not Be King*, Matthew Spalding, The Heritage Foundation, February 5, 2007.
4. https://tjrs.monticello.org/letter/58
5. *Thomas Jefferson: The Art of Power*, Jon Meacham, p. 214.
6. *Cato's Letters or Essays on Liberty, Civil and Religious, and Other Important Subjects*, Trenchard and Gordon, 1995.
7. Proverbs 16:18 (New King James Version).

8 "The Neurochemistry of Power has Implications for Political Change," *The Conversation*, February 28, 2014.

CHAPTER TWO

1 Aristotle, *Politics*, Book V.
2 https://informationpress.net/2014/06/267-founding-fathers/
3 Aristotle, *Politics*, Book VI, Section II.
4 *Ten Conservative Principles*, Russell Kirk, Russell Kirk Center for Cultural Renewal, www.kirkcenter.org.

CHAPTER THREE

1 https://rodgersandhammerstein.com/show/id-rather-be-right/
2 *1940: FDR, Wilkie, Lindbergh, Hitler—the Election amid the Storm*, Susan Dunn, p. 5.
3 See: *Grant*, Ron Chernow, pp. 899-902.
4 *Franklin Delano Roosevelt: Champion of Freedom*, Conrad Black, p. 444.
5 "Progressives Want a New Deal. The Old One Failed," George Will, *Washington Post*, August 19, 2020.
6 Quoted in *Presidential Term Limits in American History: Power, Principles, and Politics*, Michael J. Korzi, p. 101.
7 Congressional Record, 80th Congress, 1st Session, 1947, p. 1772.
8 Ibid, p. 1778.
9 "Dewey Attacks Roosevelt's Role as Indispensable," *New York Times*, September 20, 1944.
10 Congressional Record, 80th Congress, 1st Session, 1947, p. 1946.
11 Ibid., p. 1681.
12 Ibid., p. 862.
13 http://www.stanleyperthshire.co.uk/Poems

CHAPTER FOUR

1. *The Power Paradox: How We Gain and Lose Influence,* Dacher Keltner, p. 102.
2. Matthew 20:25.
3. https://www.biblehub.com/greek/1249.htm
4. *21 Laws of Leadership in the Bible: Learning to Lead from the Men and Women of Scripture,* John C. Maxwell.
5. https://press-pubs.uchicago.edu/founders/documents/
6. *Hidden History: Exploring Our Secret Past,* Daniel Boorstin, p.237.
7. https://www.texastribune.org/2023/02/01/ted-cruz-term-limits-reelection/
8. https://edmondbusiness.com/2021/02/gentlemen-this-is-a-football/

CHAPTER FIVE

1. "Scandal lobbyist Abramoff calls for term limits," Paul Bedard, *Washington Examiner*, March 22, 2016.
2. "Tommy the Cork: Washington's First Modern Lobbyist," Allan J. Lichtman, *Washington Monthly*, February 1, 1987.
3. https://www.heraldnet.com/opinion/new-permanent-campaign-steers-a-progressive-course/
4. "Lobbying Broke All-Time Mark in 2021 Amid Flurry of Government Spending," *Washington Post*, March 12, 2022.

CHAPTER SIX

1. https://www.preaching.com/articles/young-mr-spurgeon/
2. *An Outline of the Life of George Robertson,* George Robertson, p. 56.
3. I Timothy 3:1-7.
4. https://oll.libertyfund.org/title/adams-the-works-of-john-adams-vol-9-letters-and-state-papers-1799-1811
5. *Research Ties Dark Personality Traits to Political Campaigning,* https://www.susqu.edu/live/news/554-research-ties-dark-personality-traits-to-political

NOTES

6 "Marines Turned Soldiers: The Corps vs. the Army," Mackubin Thomas Owens, *National Review Online*, December 10, 2001.

7 *Strategy and Choice in Congressional Elections*, Gary C. Jacobson, p. 45.

8 https://thefulcrum.us/congress/congressional-term-limits

9 http://greatamericansongbook.net/pages/songs/n/nice_work_if_get_it_p.html

CHAPTER SEVEN

1 See: *The Making of the Great Communicator*, Ken Holden.

2 Rep. Bob Inglis (R South Carolina), "Term-limits amendment fails in House," 227-204, *Baltimore Sun*, March 30, 1995.

3 https://www.latimes.com/archives/la-xpm-1995-03-29-mn-48417-story.html

4 *The Continental Congress*, Edmund C. Burnett, p. 250.

5 https://publicpolicy.pepperdine.edu/academics/research/faculty-research/new-deal/roosevelt-speeches/fr092932.htm

6 https://www.aei.org/carpe-diem/h-l-mencken-on-elections-politics-government/

7 https://www.presidency.ucsb.edu/documents/campaign-address-the-federal-budget-pittsburgh-pennsylvania

8 https://www.pewresearch.org/politics/2023/09/19/americans-dismal-views-of-the-nations-politics/

CHAPTER EIGHT

1 *Wheels for the World: Henry Ford, His Company, and a Century of Progress*, Douglas Brinkley, p. XIV.

2 https://www.washingtonpost.com/wp-srv/politics/special/termlimits/stories/will111091.htm

3 https://professionalmotorsofwny.com/check-engine-light-what-it-means/

4 See: *Twelve Rules for Life*, Jordan Peterson.

NOTES

CHAPTER NINE

1 https://www.nytimes.com/1995/05/23/us/high-court-blocks-term-limits-for-congress-in-a-5-4-decision.html
2 Ibid.
3 https://www.gilderlehrman.org/history-resources/spotlight-primary-source/president-lincoln-first-inaugural-address-1861
4 "The Risk is Minimal': Justice Scalia On the Need for A Convention of States to Restrain Federal Power," Tom Lindsay, *Forbes*, November 11, 2019.

CHAPTER TEN

1 https://news.ballotpedia.org/2023/01/05/94-of-incumbents-won-re-election-in-2022/
2 https://www.termlimits.com/u-of-maryland-school-of-public-policy-study-advocates-for-term-limits-on-congress/https://www.cato.org/policy-analysis/will-gentlemen-please-yield-defense-constitutionality-state-imposed-term#

CHAPTER ELEVEN

1 https://www.history.com/news/has-a-u-s-supreme-court-justice-ever-been-impeached
2 https://www.usatoday.com/story/news/politics/2023/06/25/nancy-pelosi-supreme-court-term-limits-alito-thomas/70355106007/

CHAPTER TWELVE

1 https://founders.archives.gov/documents/Jefferson/01-29-02-0409
2 https://founders.archives.gov/documents/Jefferson/01-31-02-0338
3 https://crsreports.congress.gov/product/pdf/R/R47470
4 https://www.postandcourier.com/opinion/commentary/commentary-politicians-could-learn-from-mcgoverns-epiphany-on-overregulation/article_4831edae-d3cc-11ed-b9c3-7ba1408a6166.html

NOTES

5. https://www.businessinsider.com/ocasio-cortez-gets-the-economics-of-budget-deficits-job-creation-2018-7
6. https://www.apollo13minute.com/cm/episodes/minute-055-lets-work-the-problem-people/

APPENDIX

Nineteen House Members Who Voted Against Term Limits on Congress on September 28, 2023

ADAM SCHIFF	CALIFORNIA'S 30TH DISTRICT
ERIC SWALWELL	CALIFORNIA'S 14TH DISTRICT
ZOE LOFGREN	CALIFORNIA'S 18TH DISTRICT
TED LIEU	CALIFORNIA'S 36TH DISTRICT
LOU CORREA	CALIFORNIA'S 46TH DISTRICT
DARRELL ISSA	CALIFORNIA'S 48TH DISTRICT
THOMAS MCCLINTOCK	CALIFORNIA'S 5TH DISTRICT
JOSEPH NEGUSE	COLORADO'S 2ND DISTRICT
HANK JOHNSON	GEORGIA'S 4TH DISTRICT
GLENN IVEY	MARYLAND'S 4TH DISTRICT

APPENDIX

JERROLD NADLER	NEW YORK'S 12TH DISTRICT
DEBORAH ROSS	NORTH CAROLINA'S 2ND DISTRICT
MARY SCANLON	PENNSYLVANIA'S 5TH DISTRICT
STEVE COHEN	TENNESSEE'S 9TH DISTRICT
VERONICA ESCOBAR	TEXAS'S 16TH DISTRICT
SHEILA JACKSON LEE	TEXAS'S 18TH DISTRICT
BECCA BALINT	VERMONT'S AT-LARGE DISTRICT
SCOTT FITZGERALD	WISCONSIN'S 5TH DISTRICT
HARRIET HAGEMAN	WYOMING'S AT-LARGE DISTRICT

ACKNOWLEDGMENTS

WRITING MY FIRST BOOK HAS BEEN QUITE AN EXPERIENCE. I have a new appreciation for authors and editors. And I am grateful to so many wonderful people who have helped me on this journey. First, and foremost, I want to thank my wife, Carol, for her unceasing encouragement throughout the process and for her many suggestions. She is indeed the wind beneath my wings. And our daughter, Hanna, has been as encouraging and supportive as her mother. I am a blessed man.

Holly Robichaud, the Director of State Chair Program at U.S. Term Limits and a gifted strategist, has helped me too. And, of course, I would be remiss if I neglected to thank my good friend, Aaron Wright, who encouraged me to take on this project and has given me unwavering support. Thanks also to David Stokes, who has written widely on politics and history and provided vital input and editorial consultation.

U.S. Senator Tommy Tuberville and Congressman Ralph Norman were key contributors to the ideas presented in these pages—sharing their insight from Capitol Hill. Special thanks to Ralph for writing this book's foreword.

GERRICK WILKINS
OCTOBER 2023

ABOUT THE AUTHOR

After witnessing the failed policies of career politicians, the overreach of government regulations, the increased tax burden on small businesses, and the attacks on the family by the left, Gerrick Wilkins decided to take up the banner and run for Congress to represent Alabama as a servant leader. Gerrick is committed to serving a maximum of three terms in office to help restore our founding fathers' vision of a citizen legislature.

FAITH

Gerrick Wilkins took to heart the quote from President Ronald Reagan, "We can't help everyone, but everyone can help someone." This quote encouraged Gerrick to get involved in his local church, serving as a deacon and lay leader, engage in mission work locally and globally, and work with Gideons International. Gerrick is a principled man of faith and is a Christian who loves the Lord. His faith and family have encouraged him to pursue a calling to this period of civil service. Over the years, he has committed significant time and personal resources to missions and philanthropic work locally to help his community in Alabama and worldwide.

Gerrick also serves on several local advisory boards, including one for Mission Increase and Samford University's Brock School of Business.

Gerrick knows it is only by the blessings of God that our country has enjoyed bountiful prosperity. Gerrick will work hard to combat the leftist, woke agenda attacking our religious freedoms and trying to break down our family. Because of his success in the business world, Gerrick and his wife, Carol, are privileged to give substantially to churches, various charities, mission organizations, and educational programs through private donations.

FAMILY

Gerrick is a loving husband to his incredible wife of twenty-four years, Carol, and a devoted father to their amazing daughter, Hanna. Gerrick and his family moved to Alabama in 2006 and have lived in Vestavia Hills since 2014. He attended Pensacola Christian College, where he met his wife and earned a bachelor's degree in theology from Liberty University. Gerrick has been a strong proponent of lifelong learning, and during his professional career, he returned and earned a master's in business administration from Samford University.

From a young age, Gerrick has been interested in how our country is governed, working on several local campaigns while in high school. After working a lifetime to build a successful career, Gerrick has been disheartened with the direction of our nation, prompting him to write this book on congressional term limits and the problem of career politicians.

PHILOSOPHY

Gerrick is an American business leader with over twenty-four years of private sector experience in the automotive industry. His experience managing large-scale dealerships and helping other community-based dealers grow has allowed him to earn great success and achieve the American dream. During his time managing dealerships in Alabama, Gerrick has learned firsthand of the constant heartaches small businesses must contend with from overregulation and excessive tax policies. Gerrick's real-world experience allows him to understand the challenges business owners face daily.

Gerrick believes we need citizens to stand up and say, "We don't want career politicians anymore. We want citizen lawmakers." It is time for us to end the cycle of corruption fueled by lifelong careers in government. Our country needs a change now.

MY TERM LIMITS PLEDGE

U.S. Term Limits Amendment Pledge

I, __Gerrick Wilkins__, pledge that as a member of Congress I will cosponsor and vote for the U.S. Term Limits Amendment of three (3) House terms and two (2) Senate terms and no longer limit.

(signature) 10-2-23
(Candidate Signature, Date)

Gerrick Wilkins
(Candidate name printed)

(signature)
(Witness Signature)

Aaron Wright
(Witness name printed)

U.S. Term Limits / 2955 Pineda Plaza Way Suite 226 / Melbourne, Fla. 32940
Pledges can be texted to (321) 345-7455 or emailed to press@termlimits.com

★ ★ ★

For further insights and to actively participate in
the vital movement for congressional term limits,
I highly recommend visiting:

termlimits.com